THE GREAT AUSTIE

Australia
1788-1988

1788–1988 THE AUSTRALIAN BICENTENNIAL

Any profits from the sale of this book will go to the West Midlands Branch of the Britain–Australia Bicentennial Committee to help provide funds for an annual scholarship to Australia for a young person.

THE GREAT AUSTRALIAN BITE

Annabel Bevan

COLLINS
PUBLISHERS
AUSTRALIA

COLLINS PUBLISHERS AUSTRALIA

© 1988 Annabel Bevan

Edited by Lynn Brodie

National Library of Australia
Cataloguing-in-Publication data:

    The Great Australian Bite.

        Includes index.
        ISBN 0 7322 2464 0.

            1. Cookery. I. Bevan, Annabel.

641.5

All rights reserved. No part of this publication may be reproduced, stored in a retrieval system, or transmitted, in any form, or by any means, electronic, mechanical, photocopying, recording or otherwise, without the prior permission of the publishers.

This book is sold subject to the condition that it shall not, by way of trade or otherwise, be lent, resold, hired out or otherwise circulated without the publisher's prior consent in a form of binding or cover other than that in which it is published and without a similar condition including this condition being imposed on the subsequent purchaser.

Designed and typeset in Goudy Oldstyle by Brodie Commercial Services Pty Limited, Sydney

Printed by Mandarin Offset, Hong Kong

COMPILER'S NOTES

What could I possibly do to help raise money for a Bicentennial Exchange Scheme? Somehow I found myself — an Australian living in England — on the West Midlands Committee of the Britain–Australia Bicentennial Committee. There we were, sitting around a table and racking our brains for ideas. I like cooking and rather tentatively suggested that a cookery book might be a good idea. 'Over to you,' they said, and so off I went to write to one or two well-known people to see whether they would contribute to a sort of 'celebrity recipe collection'.

From there on things snowballed. A title was dreamed up, the Prince of Wales sent a recipe, closely followed by Bob Hawke and Margaret Thatcher. By July 1987 we ended up with a huge pile of correspondence and the problems of putting it all together. Mercifully Collins came to the rescue and here, eighteen months after its conception, is *The Great Australian Bite*.

I should emphasise that it is *not* meant to be a collection of either Australian or British recipes. It is a hotchpotch of personal contributions and by no means comprehensive. But I hope it will be fun to use: it is meant to be the personalities' favourite recipes, and as such they may provide some interesting talking points at dinner!

A project like this would get nowhere, of course, without the help and encouragement of many people. Particularly the West Midlands Committee of the BABC have provided support: Gaye Hawnt helped collect recipes and Glenice Carver thought up the title. At Shrewsbury Simon Baxter, Sue Kirk and Dee Dakers have all helped with typing, collating recipes and writing letters. Finally, I really wouldn't have got going without Anne Ager's positive and helpful advice when the first recipes started coming in.

Bon appetit.

ANNABEL BEVAN
Shrewsbury, August 1987

Contents

Ita Buttrose OBE	9
Anne D Ager	19
A La Carte Magazine	21
Julie Anthony OBE	24
Sallyanne Atkinson	25
Australian High Commission, London	26
Tony Barber	28
Graeme Bell	29
Senator Lady Bjelke-Petersen	29
Blue Peter (BBC)	31
Rabbi Lionel Blue	32
Alan Bond	33
Sir Donald Bradman	34
Brown Brothers Milawa Vineyard	34
Max Bygraves	37
Robert Carrier	38
Pat Cash	40
Charles, HRH The Prince of Wales	41
Diane Cilento	42
Country Living Magazine	43
The Country Women's Association of Victoria	46
Nicola Cox	47
Cranks Health Foods	49
Hector Crawford	51
Josceline Dimbleby	53
Ken Done	54
Ed Doolan	55
The Dorchester	56
Elizabeth Durack CMG, OBE	57
Mary Durack	58
John Eley	59
Eton College	59
Keith Floyd	60
Mem Fox	61
The Rt Hon. Malcolm Fraser CH	62

Tony Greig	63
Jo Griffiths	64
Anne Haddy	68
Rolf Harris	69
Bob Hawke	70
Ken Hom	71
Frank Ifield	73
Alan Jones	74
Bernard King	75
Rustie Lee	77
Judy McCallum	79
Leo McKern	80
Keith Michell	81
National Trust of Australia (Victoria)	82
John Newcombe	82
Bert Newton	83
Patti Newton	84
Greg Norman	85
Kerry Packer	86
Sara Paston-Williams	89
Eric Pearce	93
Jean Penman	94
The Ritz	95
Barbara Ronay	100
Rosalind Runcie	101
Shrewsbury School	102
Maureen Simpson	102
James Smillie	105
Delia Smith	106
Michael Smith	106
Daryl Somers	107
Mary Steele	108
Sir Ninian Stephen	110
Jan Stephenson	111
Dame Joan Sutherland	112
Beverley Sutherland Smith	113

Maggie Tabberer	115
Nick Tate	116
Margaret Thatcher	117
Brigitte Tilleray	118
Adele Weiss	120
Western Australia House, London	122
Terry Wogan	126
Cliff Young	126
Index	127

ITA BUTTROSE OBE (Australia)
Editor-in-Chief, *Sun–Herald*, and author

> I've put together a Bicentennial Banquet. Dishes can be served as a buffet, or you can choose the ones you most like and turn them into a three-course dinner party. It's up to you. I think there is enough variety to cater for most tastes.

Bicentennial Banquet

Menu

Iced Minted Green Pea Soup
Prawns and Oysters with Mrs Doyle's Cocktail Sauce
Egg and Bacon Pie
Carpetbag Steak
Carpetbag Sausages
Australian Roast Lamb with Mint Glazed Pears
Baked Tasmanian Atlantic Salmon
Beppi's Mozzarella Salad and Basil Sauce
Avocado and Grapefruit Salad
Queensland Salad
Salad of Many Lettuces
Baked Snake
Damper
Pumpkin Scones
Governor Phillip's Rum Pie
Mum's Fruit Salad
Little Lamingtons and Coffee

Iced Minted Green Pea Soup

4 cups good chicken stock
500 g (1 lb) frozen minted green peas
seasonings
300 ml (½ pint) cream
300 ml (½ pint) milk

Cook frozen peas in chicken stock. Cool. Puree in blender. Add salt and pepper to taste. Add cream and enough milk to make soup desired thickness. Blend again and chill. Serve garnished with freshly chopped mint or paprika.

If you are serving at the table then obviously soup can be put in bowls. If outdoors, I suggest you serve in teacups or mugs — it's the easiest way to drink it!

Prawns and Oysters

No Australian Bicentennial Banquet would be a true-blue dinki-di affair without fresh prawns and rock oysters. Just arrange them on a plate, be sure to have them very well chilled, and serve with a tasty cocktail sauce.

Cocktail Sauce

My favourite cocktail sauce is from Mrs Alice Doyle, whose family runs the best seafood restaurant in Sydney — Doyle's — on the harbour front at Watsons Bay.

½ cup mayonnaise
½ cup tomato sauce
½ small tin reduced cream
2 teaspoons Worcestershire sauce
1 tablespoon brown vinegar or lemon juice
1 teaspoon horse-radish sauce
freshly ground pepper
salt
pinch basil
parsley, finely chopped
dash tabasco sauce

This is the simplest of sauces to make. Just shake all the ingredients thoroughly, or mix in a blender. Serve. If you like garlic, add crushed garlic to taste.

Egg and Bacon Pie

500 g (1 lb) flour
185 g (6 oz) butter or dripping
1 egg yolk
2 teaspoons lemon juice
¼ cup cold water
1 tablespoon sugar
strips of bacon
eggs
pepper and salt

Sift flour, add butter and mix in with a knife or fingertips. Add yolk of egg, lemon juice and water beaten together. Knead lightly and roll up (only roll out once). Line dish (a sandwich tin will do) with half the pastry. Bake in moderate oven 20–30 minutes.

Sprinkle pastry lightly with flour. Cut strips of bacon and cover bottom of dish. Break in as many eggs as required. Add pepper and salt. Cover with pastry and bake in moderate oven for ¾ hour.

Carpetbag Steak

Thickly cut slices of beef stuffed with oysters was particularly common in early Australia. It can be barbecued (my favourite way of cooking) or grilled in the oven.

2 x 750 g (1½ lb) pieces whole beef fillet
salt and freshly ground black pepper
20 fresh oysters
2 tablespoons oil
½ small onion, finely chopped
1 tablespoon lemon juice
1 tablespoon finely chopped parsley
2 tablespoons dry sherry

Trim the steak of any surplus fat. With a sharp knife cut a pocket into each fillet, taking care not to cut through to the other side. Season the pocket with salt and pepper and stuff each fillet with 10 oysters. Tie each fillet with string and secure oysters in place with a small skewer.

Make a marinade by combining the remaining ingredients. Place the fillets in a shallow pan or dish and pour the marinade over them. Allow to stand for 1 hour, turning from time to time.

Place the whole fillets on the barbecue and cook until brown on all sides. Remove the fillets from the barbecue and cut into 2.5 cm (1 inch) thick slices. Return to the barbecue and cook each slice according to individual taste.

Serves 6

Carpetbag Sausages

As many sausages as you require — pork or beef, whatever your preference. Bake in oven or on barbecue until cooked. Slit and stuff with fresh oysters.

These are perfect for starters or can be eaten as part of the main course. Suit yourself. But be prepared — your guests will want more . . . and more!

Australian Roast Lamb with Mint Glazed Pears

Many thanks to Dorothy Siller of the Sydney suburb of Avalon for her recipe for Mint Glazed Pears, which she says (and having tried it, I agree) goes well with roast lamb. Australian lamb is always delicious and appeals to all palates. You can cook it until very well done, or for a lesser period and serve the lamb pink. I prefer the latter.

Mint Glazed Pears

250 g (8 oz) jar mint jelly
½ cup white vinegar
¼ cup light corn syrup
1 large can pears, drained
½ teaspoon mint extract

Put the mint jelly, vinegar and corn syrup in a pot and simmer 15 minutes until jelly is dissolved. Put in the pears and mint extract. Simmer about 15 minutes more until the pears absorb the flavour and take on a green tint. Be careful not to overcook otherwise pears will break up.

Baked Tasmanian Atlantic Salmon

Tasmanian Atlantic salmon is one of the newest taste treats on the Australian menu. It is farm-bred and produced at Dover, about a ninety-minute drive south from Hobart. Tasmanians say it is superior to, or at least as good as, fresh Scottish or Canadian salmon. It is quite delicious.

1 whole fish, 1–1½ kg (2–3 lb)
olive oil
½ cup champagne

Cut a piece of aluminium foil about 15 cm (6 inches) longer than the fish and paint thoroughly with olive oil. Put foil on baking dish or large scone tray. Place fish, lightly seasoned with salt, in middle of oiled foil.

Take up edges of foil and make it into a boat shape around fish before pouring in champagne. Twist the edges of the foil together securely, right along the fish and at the head and tail, so not a drop of juice is lost.

Pre-heat oven to 125°C (250°F, Gas Mark ½) and put fish on tray in oven. Cook a 1 kg (2 lb) fish for 1 hour. Don't be tempted to open the oven or fiddle with the foil while it cooks.

When the fish is cooked put it straight on to the serving dish, open up foil and slide the foil off the fish, being careful not to spill any of the juices.

Cool and serve. The fish can be baked the day before, but is more delicious if cooked and let cool for about 2 hours before the meal.

Beppi's Mozzarella Salad and Basil Sauce

Australia's cuisine has changed considerably since the end of World War Two because of the many European migrants who settled here. The Italians introduced us to olives, wonderful veal dishes and spaghetti! They also showed us a thing or two about salads. No Bicentennial Banquet would be complete without a contribution from the people from other lands who now make up Australia.

Beppi's, in Sydney's Yurong Street, was one of the earliest and best Italian restaurants. It began in 1956. In those days Beppi had to offer unadventurous Australians a free sample of his menu to get us to try such delicacies as octopus. Now he can hardly keep up with the demand.

This salad is one I especially enjoy.

slices of tomato
1 basil leaf
Bocconcini cheese (made from goat or buffalo milk)
chopped basil
fresh oregano
mustard
little bit of garlic
red wine vinegar
olive and safflower oil
freshly ground pepper
1 fillet of anchovy on top

Combine all ingredients according to taste. Beppi mixes everything together and then adds more of anything if needed.

Note: If you have trouble getting Bocconcini cheese, substitute Mozzarella.

Avocado and Grapefruit Salad

avocados — allow half per person
lemon
fresh grapefruit
mayonnaise
heart of lettuce
walnuts, chopped

Peel, seed and cut avocados into 1.5 cm (½ inch) cubes. Squeeze a lemon over peeled cubes to stop them from discolouring. Add an equal quantity of peeled, seeded grapefruit broken into segments. Stir in small amount of creamy mayonnaise — gently, so that avocado is not mashed. Ladle into heart of lettuce leaves. Garnish with chopped walnuts.

Queensland Salad

This recipe comes from a splendid Colonial Cookbook *put together by the Jondaryan Women's Auxiliary to raise funds for the Jondaryan Woolshed Association, Queensland. It's perfect on a hot Australia Day.*

4 large bananas, sliced
1 tablespoon lemon juice
3 cups cooked rice, cooled
1 large red apple, cored and chopped
125 g (4 oz) sultana grapes (or seeded green grapes)
90 g (3 oz) pineapple chunks
2 tablespoons (½ oz) chopped walnuts
1 tablespoon chopped chives
2 tablespoons (½ oz) desiccated coconut

Mix ingredients, pour dressing over and sprinkle with coconut.

Dressing
½ cup mayonnaise
2 tablespoons lemon juice
¼ teaspoon chilli powder
½ teaspoon dry mustard

Mix all ingredients together well and use.

Salad of Many Lettuces

lettuces
green capsicum
chives
dressing

Buy a selection of lettuces — there are many varieties available. Wash and arrange attractively in a salad bowl. Chop up capsicum (one or more, depending on the number you're serving) and chives. Mix up your favourite dressing (which I trust includes garlic!) and pour over it.

Baked Snake
(Courtesy Rowntrees Restaurant)

Some of you may like to try a 'real' Australian recipe. Of course you first have to catch your snake. No, I don't know how you do that. Good luck!

1 snake — brown or black or carpet — about 183 cm (6 feet) long with a 7.5 cm (3 inch) girth
2 people
an open fire
length of string

The two people need to sit one each side of the open fire and stretch the snake over the heat. Sear the snake all over by turning it several times and stretching it until it is cooked evenly from head to tail (this keeps the juices in the snake).

Make an incision on both sides of the spinal cord, right down to the bone, about 1.5 cm (½ inch) deep. Roll the snake as you would a ribbed roast — in a coil. Tie it securely. Then cover it with hot coals from the fire so that it is completely covered. Cook for about 20 minutes on one side, then turn it over and cook for another 10 minutes. Then remove the entrails.

The Aborigines cook the entrails in the snake because they believe in cooking the whole reptile for religious reasons. They then eat the entrails; but John Paul from Rowntrees suggests removing them.

Serve with a Rosella Sauce, which has a lovely plummy flavour. Pick the little Rosella buds. Strip the petals off and stew them as you would a fruit, using lots of sugar as the Rosella is quite bitter. There is plenty of pectin in the Rosella so it goes into quite a jammy consistency.

Damper

Damper was part of the Australian diet from the very early days of our settlement by the British. There is nothing better than hot damper spread with butter. Originally it was made by winding the damper around a stick and cooking it over an open fire in the outback. Camp cooks made dampers in heavy cast-iron pots or in the glowing embers of the fire.

4 cups (1 lb) self-raising flour
2 cups water or milk (sour milk is best — it gives a soft texture and milk helps the keeping qualities of the damper)
1 teaspoon salt

Toss in all the ingredients and mix to a gooey lump that leaves the side of the bowl. Turn out on to a floured board. Turn edges into centre and turn over so that you have a smooth top. Shape the damper, place on a floured baking tray and place in oven heated to 200°C (400°F, Gas Mark 6). Cook for 45 minutes.

Pumpkin Scones

Pumpkin scones have become a part of Australian folklore because of Senator Lady Flo Bjelke-Petersen, wife of Queensland's longest serving and controversial Premier Sir Joh Bjelke-Petersen (who stepped down in late 1987). They are one of her favourite dishes. She often whips up a batch of pumpkin scones, and guests always ask for more. For a Bicentennial Banquet to be truly representative of all Australia, pumpkin scones are a must. Use them as a bread roll substitute.

See page 30

Governor Phillip's Rum Pie

Governor Phillip was Australia's first governor and he was a man who liked his food, especially his puddings! Rum was the colony's popular drink. Governor Phillip liked his rum in a pie.

Pastry
1½ cups (6 oz) plain flour
60 g (2 oz) butter
1 teaspoon sugar
2 tablespoons hot water

Sift flour and rub in butter. Dissolve sugar in hot water before adding to flour mixture. Mix to a soft dough and chill 15–20 minutes. Roll out and line 20 cm (8 inch) pie dish. Cook in hot oven, 200°C (400°F, Gas Mark 6), for 15 minutes. Allow to cool before filling.

Rum Cream Filling
3 egg yolks
1 tablespoon soft butter
½ cup (4 oz) sugar
2 teaspoons gelatine
¼ cup cold water
300 ml (½ pint) cream
¼ cup dark rum

Beat egg yolks and butter, gradually add sugar and beat until frothy. In saucepan soften gelatine in water and bring to boil over low heat. Slowly pour into egg mixture, beating well all the time. Whip cream until stiff and fold into egg mixture, then gently fold in rum. Refrigerate until stiff enough to form peaks when dropped from spoon, then heap into crust and chill 3–4 hours before serving. Decorate with chocolate shavings.

Mum's Fruit Salad

You might prefer a lighter dessert than Governor Phillip's Rum Pie. My mother makes the best fruit salad. Guests always want more.

1 watermelon
rockmelon
cherries
sultana grapes
strawberries
passionfruit
any other fruit of your choice

Scoop the fruit out of the watermelon, remove seeds, then dice and put back in the watermelon shells. Add remaining fruits. Splash over some sherry. Serve well chilled.

Lamingtons

Lamingtons are usually served for morning or afternoon tea. But for our Bicentennial Banquet I suggest you serve them with coffee. It is believed lamingtons were named after Lord Lamington, Governor of Queensland 1895–1901.

28 x 18 cm (11 x 7 inch) sponge cake
¼ cup (3 oz) strawberry jam
¾ cup thickened (double) cream, whipped
chocolate glace icing
1½ cups (4½ oz) desiccated coconut

Split the sponge cake in two lengthwise and remove the top layer. Spread the bottom layer with jam and whipped cream. Place the top layer back on. Cut the cake into small squares. Dip the cakes into the chocolate icing and, using a fork, roll in desiccated coconut.

Chocolate Glace Icing
1 cup (5 oz) icing sugar
2 tablespoons cocoa
2 tablespoons boiling water

Sift together icing sugar and cocoa, gradually add water and beat to a smooth paste.
Makes 8

ANNE D AGER (Britain)
Cookery expert

Seafood and Soft Cheese Lasagne

500 g (1 lb) fresh spinach, cooked
freshly ground nutmeg
salt and freshly ground black pepper
3 tablespoons *fromage blanc*
1 clove garlic, peeled and crushed
125 g (4 oz) prawns, cooked and peeled
125 g (4 oz) mussels, cooked and shelled
1 egg yolk
250 g (8 oz) dried green lasagne (the variety that needs no pre-cooking)
125 g (4 oz) low-fat soft cheese
150 ml (¼ pint) thick natural yoghurt
1 egg, beaten
2 tablespoons grated Parmesan cheese
sprigs fresh herbs to garnish

Mix the spinach with nutmeg, salt and pepper to taste; stir in the *fromage blanc*, garlic, prawns, mussels and egg yolk.

Put half the spinach mixture in a lightly greased deep ovenproof dish and top with half the lasagne. Add the soft cheese in small knobs, top with the remaining spinach mixture and then the lasagne.

Mix the yoghurt with the beaten egg and spoon over the top layer of lasagne; sprinkle with the grated Parmesan cheese.

Bake at 190°C (375°F, Gas Mark 5) for 35–40 minutes, until bubbling and golden.

Serve piping hot wedges, garnished with herbs, together with a salad.
Serves 6

Salmon in Vine Leaves

1 x 2 kg (4 lb) salmon or sea trout, head and tail removed, filleted but not skinned
salt and freshly ground black pepper
90 g (3 oz) curd cheese
1 clove garlic, peeled and crushed
rind 1 lemon, finely grated
2 tablespoons chopped fresh dill
10 vine leaves, soaked in warm water for 10 minutes and drained
300 ml (½ pint) dry white wine
1 lemon, thinly sliced
thin slices lemon or lime to garnish

Lay out the fish fillets flesh side uppermost and season with salt and pepper.

Mix the curd cheese with the garlic, lemon rind and dill; spread over one fish fillet and lay the second fillet on the top. Wrap the 'sandwiched fish' in vine leaves so as to completely enclose it.

Lay the wrapped fish in an ovenproof dish and pour over the wine; add the lemon slices and cover with foil. Bake at 190°C (375°F, Gas Mark 5) for 45 minutes. Meanwhile, make the sauce.

Lift the fish carefully out of the baking dish and place on a long oval platter; garnish with slices of lemon or lime.

To serve, fold back the vine leaves and cut through the stuffed fish in sections. Serve accompanied by the sauce.

Serves 6–8

Sauce
150 ml (¼ pint) thick natural yoghurt
1 tablespoon orange lumpfish roe
1 tablespoon chopped fresh dill

Mix the yoghurt with the lumpfish roe and dill; season to taste.

A LA CARTE Magazine © (Britain)

Scallop Salad with Asparagus

4 new potatoes
12 small scallops
1 bunch asparagus
3 types of lettuce

Dressing
150 ml (¼ pint) light olive oil
100 ml (3 fl. oz) tarragon vinegar
1 teaspoon lemon juice
salt
freshly ground black pepper

Wipe the new potatoes and put into boiling salted water for 10–12 minutes until cooked.

Steam the scallops and the asparagus for 10 minutes, and while they are cooking start to prepare the salad.

First make the dressing. Mix the olive oil with the vinegar and the lemon juice, seasoning to taste.

Wash the lettuces and divide among four plates. Slice the potatoes, then arrange the warm scallops, asparagus and potatoes among the leaves, drizzle the dressing over the salad, and serve immediately.

Serves 4

Lamb en Croute with Fresh Figs and Ginger

Boned loin of lamb stuffed with fresh figs and ginger, wrapped in pastry coated with sesame seeds, and a sauce flavoured with ginger wine — it all adds up to an unusually seductive dish.

1 large loin of lamb, about 1 kg (2½ lb) before boning
1 stick of celery, roughly chopped
1 carrot, sliced
1 onion, unpeeled and roughly chopped
30 g (1 oz) butter
1 small leek, trimmed and chopped
5 fresh figs, finely chopped
2.5 cm (1 inch) length fresh ginger, peeled and finely chopped
30 g (1 oz) Brazil-nuts, chopped
¼ cup (½ oz) breadcrumbs
1 tablespoon chopped fresh parsley
salt
freshly ground black pepper
375 g (13 oz) packet puff pastry
beaten egg to glaze
1 tablespoon sesame seeds
100 ml (3 fl. oz) ginger wine
100 ml (3 fl. oz) thickened (double) cream
2–3 fresh figs to garnish

Get your butcher to bone the lamb and ask for the bones. Pre-heat the oven at 220°C (425°F, Gas Mark 7) and brown the bones for 15 minutes. Place in a pan with the celery, carrot, onion and 900 ml (1½ pints) water. Bring to the boil, reduce the heat and simmer for 2–3 hours, skimming off fat and scum when necessary. Strain, return to the saucepan and boil to reduce to 150 ml (¼ pint).

Melt the butter in a frying-pan, add the leek. Fry for 5 minutes, then stir in the figs, ginger, Brazil-nuts, breadcrumbs, parsley and seasoning.

Place the lamb, skin side down, on a board. Spread the stuffing down the centre and roll up the meat, securing at 2.5 cm (1 inch) intervals with string. Place in a roasting tin and cook at 220°C (425°F, Gas Mark 7) for 15 minutes. Drain off all but 1 tablespoon of the juices and set aside the roasting tin. Leave the meat to cool then remove the string.

Roll out the pastry thinly and brush the edges with beaten egg. Place the meat in the centre of the pastry and bring the pastry over the meat to enclose it completely, trimming off excess pastry at the ends. Transfer to a dampened baking tray with the join underneath. Score a diamond pattern on the pastry, brush with beaten egg and sprinkle with sesame seeds. Cook for 15 minutes at 220°C (425°F, Gas Mark 7). Reduce the heat to 180°C (350°F, Gas Mark 4) and cook for a further 40 minutes for rare or 1 hour for medium, covering with foil if the pastry gets brown.

Towards the end of the cooking time add the reduced stock, ginger wine and cream to the roasting juices in the tin and cook until the mixture thinly coats the back of a wooden spoon. Season to taste.

Slice the lamb and serve with a little of the sauce. Garnish each plate with half a fresh fig, cut in a fan shape.

Serves 4–6

Bread and Butter Pudding

Liqueur-steeped fruit, golden baked bread, creamy vanilla custard — an irresistible pudding like nothing mother ever made.

90 g (3 oz) sultanas
2 tablespoons Amaretto or Cointreau
300 ml (½ pint) milk
¼ cup (2 oz) castor sugar
1 vanilla pod
3 eggs
150 ml (¼ pint) thickened (double) cream
8 thin slices white bread, generously buttered
¼ cup apricot jam
shredded almonds, toasted
icing sugar for dusting

Place the sultanas in a bowl with the Amaretto or Cointreau and leave to soak for 6 hours or overnight.

Pour the milk into a saucepan with the sugar and vanilla pod. Bring the mixture slowly to the boil, then leave it to cool. Remove the vanilla pod (this can be lightly rinsed, dried and stored for future use). Beat together the eggs and cream, gradually blending in the milk mixture.

Make sandwiches of the bread using half the apricot jam. Trim off the crusts and cut each sandwich diagonally into four. Alternatively, cut two 5 cm (2 inch) rounds from each sandwich using a pastry cutter. Keep the rounds for the top layer and use the trimmings in the base of the dish. Arrange the bread in layers in a 1.2 litre (2 pint) ovenproof serving dish, sprinkling each layer with the fruit.

Gradually pour the cream mixture over the bread, making sure all the bread is coated. Leave the pudding to stand for between 30 minutes and 1 hour (this allows the bread to absorb the liquid so it becomes light and crisp during cooking).

Place the dish in a roasting tin and fill the tin to a depth of 2.5 cm (1 inch) with hot water. Bake the pudding at 160°C (325°F, Gas Mark 3) for about 50 minutes to 1 hour until the top is crisp and golden.

Meanwhile, press the remaining apricot jam through a sieve into a saucepan. Add 1 tablespoon water and melt gently. Brush the jam over the pudding and sprinkle with toasted almonds. Dredge lightly with icing sugar.

Bread and Butter Pudding is best served warm rather than hot.

Serves 4-6

JULIE ANTHONY OBE (Australia)
Entertainer

Great Carrot Wedding Cake

This Australian recipe, which I baked for Jon Pertwee a number of times while we were at the Adelphi together, was a particular favourite of his.

3 cups (12 oz) wholewheat pastry flour
1 teaspoon baking soda
1 teaspoon baking powder
2 cups (14 oz) raw sugar
½ teaspoon salt
1 cup vegetable oil
4 eggs, beaten
3 cups grated carrot
½ cup (2 oz) chopped walnuts or pecans
½ cup (3 oz) raisins
½ cup (3 oz) chopped pitted dates
½ cup (1 oz) shredded coconut
1 cup mashed bananas
1 cup crushed fresh pineapple
1 teaspoon vanilla
1 teaspoon cinnamon

Sift together flour, baking soda, baking powder, sugar and salt. Beat in vegetable oil and eggs.

Stir in carrots, nuts, raisins, dates, coconut, bananas and pineapple. Season with vanilla and cinnamon.

Grease a shallow rectangular baking pan about 31 x 23 cm (12 x 9 inches) and a shallow pan about 23 x 20 cm (9 x 8 inches). Pour cake batter into both pans and bake in a 160°C (325°F, Gas Mark 3) oven for 1 hour or until done.
Let cake cool for 45 minutes; remove and spread with icing.

Icing
375 g (12 oz) cream cheese, softened
1 cup (5 oz) icing sugar

Beat cream cheese and sugar together until smooth. Spread icing over top and sides of each cake layer. Centre the smaller layer on top of the larger.

SALLYANNE ATKINSON (Australia)
Lord Mayor of Brisbane

Pavlova

4 egg whites
pinch salt
250 g (8 oz) castor sugar
whipped cream and fruit to decorate

1 teaspoon vinegar
½ teaspoon vanilla essence
2 teaspoons cornflour

Beat the egg whites with a pinch of salt for 5–6 minutes, gradually adding the castor sugar, vinegar and vanilla essence. Beat until stiff. Fold in cornflour lightly.
Dampen the surface of the pavlova plate and heap mixture on to the damp surface.
If using *electric oven*, pre-heat to 200°C (400°F) then set at 120°C (250°F) and bake undisturbed for 1½ hours. *No longer.*
If using *gas oven*, bake for 10 minutes at 200°C (400°F, Gas Mark 6) then for a further 1 hour turned to low.
Top pavlova with whipped cream and decorate with fruit as desired. Recommended are: fruit salad, passionfruit, sliced strawberries, crushed pineapple, bananas.

AUSTRALIAN HIGH COMMISSION, London

Stuffed Pears

6 small macaroons
1 egg yolk
grated rind of 1 orange
1–2 teaspoons sherry or Marsala
3 large pears

½ cup white wine
2 teaspoons brown sugar
150 ml (¼ pint) sour cream
brown sugar to taste

Crush macaroons and mix with egg yolk, grated rind and sherry. Peel pears, cut in half and remove cores, stuff pear halves with macaroon mixture and place in a baking dish. Mix wine and sugar together and pour over pears. Bake in a moderate oven until cooked (approximately 40 minutes). Mix sour cream with sugar. Serve with the warm pears.

Note: Apricots can be used in place of pears.

Avocado Cocktail

6 rashers streaky bacon
¼ cup mayonnaise
½–1 small tub sour cream
squeeze lemon juice

185 g (6 oz) prawns, cooked
lettuce
2 avocado pears
lemon slices for decoration

Cook bacon until very crisp; allow to cool and break into small pieces. Mix mayonnaise with sour cream and lemon juice to taste. Devein fresh prawns, or simply thaw frozen ones. Add to dressing with the bacon. Shred lettuce and place small amount in six individual glass dishes. Skin and dice avocado and add to the mayonnaise and bacon dressing. Spoon equal amounts into the dishes over the lettuce. Garnish with lemon slices.
Serves 6

Note: Make no more than 30 minutes before serving.

Crunchies

½ cup (2 oz) plain flour
½ cup (4 oz) granulated sugar
2 cups (6 oz) rolled oats
1 teaspoon bicarbonate of soda
1 tablespoon golden syrup
125 g (4 oz) margarine

Mix flour, sugar, oats and soda together. Cook syrup and margarine together and bring to the boil, add to the dry ingredients and mix thoroughly. Spread evenly over a baking tin and bake for the first 30 minutes in a moderate oven, and then for 30 minutes in a slow oven. Cut into pieces whilst still warm.

Jaffa Lamingtons

Cake
1 cup (4 oz) self-raising flour
¼ cup (1 oz) custard powder
1 cup (7 oz) sugar
½ cup milk

2 eggs
125 g (4 oz) butter, softened
1 teaspoon vanilla
1 tablespoon grated orange rind

Chocolate Coating
3 cups (1 lb 6 oz) crystal sugar
⅓ cup (1 oz) cocoa
1 cup water

1 teaspoon vanilla
coconut

Passionfruit Cream
300 ml (½ pint) cream

410 g (13 oz) passionfruit pulp

Sift flour and custard powder into small mixer bowl. Add remaining cake ingredients, beat on medium speed 6 minutes.
Pour mixture into a greased and lined 28 x 18 cm (11 x 7 inch) lamington pan. Bake in a slow oven 150°C (300°F, Gas Mark 2) for 40 minutes. Stand 3 minutes before turning out. When cold, cut cake into 24 pieces.
Put sugar, cocoa and water into a saucepan, stir occasionally till boiling. Remove from heat, brush down sides of saucepan with a wet pastry brush. Return coating to heat — *do not stir again*. Boil gently for 10 minutes.
Remove from heat, add vanilla, stir 1 minute. Cool slightly. Dip cakes quickly in coating, toss in coconut. Allow coating to dry.
Beat cream, fold in passionfruit. Slit lamingtons, fill, and top with cream to serve if desired.
Makes 24

TONY BARBER (Australia)
Television personality

Tony Barber's 'Porky Dogs'

frankfurt sausages
bacon rashers

Take any number of frankfurt sausages (the fatter the better). Parboil the frankfurts. Slice down but not through. Insert sliced bacon rashers in each slit; grill under medium heat for 8–10 minutes.

Serve in rolls, with bread, or eat with fingers.

Steak and Kidney Pie

1 kg (2 lb) stewing steak
12 lamb kidneys
1 large onion, chopped
flour

Cut steak and kidney into chunks. Mix in the chopped onion. Season with salt and pepper and roll in flour. Cover with water. Simmer in oven (medium heat) for 1½ hours.

Place pastry over meat and bake for another 10 minutes.

Serve with cooked carrots, turnips and potatoes.

Pastry
1 cup (4 oz) flour
¼ teaspoon salt
90 g (3 oz) butter or lard
water to mix

Combine flour, salt, butter and water; mix to breadcrumb texture. Roll out.

GRAEME BELL of Graeme Bell All-Stars (Australia)
Jazz musician

Mother Bell's Custard

Graeme's mother used to make this when we stayed with her shortly after we were married, and when I commented on how delicious it was she gave me the recipe. It remains a firm favourite in this family. Dorothy Bell

1 egg
1 tablespoon cornflour
1 tablespoon sugar

1½ cups milk
knob of butter
nutmeg

Beat the egg well into the cornflour and sugar.

Rinse saucepan in hot water and boil the milk in it. Pour milk on to the other ingredients in a basin. Stir and pour into saucepan. Slowly bring to boil. Simmer 3 minutes, stirring to prevent lumps. Take away from heat, put in the knob of butter and stir in well.

Turn into dish, sprinkle with nutmeg, and allow to cool before putting in refrigerator.

You can decorate the custard with slices of kiwi-fruit (Chinese gooseberries). It is usually served with stewed fruit.

SENATOR LADY (FLORENCE) BJELKE-PETERSEN (Australia)
Senator for Queensland

Sago Pudding

2 tablespoons sago
1 cup milk
1 tablespoon butter
1 cup (5 oz) brown sugar
1 egg

1 cup (5 oz) raisins
1 cup (2 oz) fresh breadcrumbs
1 teaspoon soda
1 tablespoon milk
pinch salt

Soak sago in milk overnight.

Beat butter and sugar, add egg. Then add sago, followed by raisins and breadcrumbs. Dissolve soda in milk and stir into mixture. Add salt. Cook in steamer for 3 hours.

Flo's Pumpkin Scones

1 tablespoon butter
½ cup (4 oz) sugar
¼ teaspoon salt

1 egg
1 cup mashed pumpkin, cold
2–2¼ cups (approx. 8 oz) self-raising flour, sifted

Beat in mixer the butter, sugar and salt; add egg and pumpkin. Fold in the flour by hand.
Cook at 230°C (450°F, Gas Mark 8) on top shelf of oven for about 15–20 minutes.

Florence's Anzac Biscuits with Peanuts

2 teaspoons syrup
125 g (4 oz) butter
1 heaped teaspoon baking soda
1½ cups (5 oz) rolled oats
1 cup (4 oz) self-raising flour

1 cup (7 oz) sugar
1 cup (3 oz) desiccated coconut
½ cup (2 oz) chopped peanuts
1 egg (not beaten)
pinch salt

Melt together the syrup, butter and baking soda. Mix remaining ingredients together. Add melted ingredients and mix well. Knead for 5 minutes. Roll into small pieces and place on greased tin. Cook for about 15–20 minutes in a moderate oven.

Sponge Cake

4 eggs, separated
1 cup (7 oz) sugar
¼ teaspoon salt
¾ cup (3 oz) cornflour
¼ cup (1 oz) plain flour

1 teaspoon cream of tartar
½ teaspoon baking soda
1 teaspoon butter
2 teaspoons hot milk

Beat the egg whites well. Add the sugar and salt, then the egg yolks. Sift the dry ingredients, add by hand. Dissolve the butter in the hot milk and fold in. Cook at 190°C (375°F, Gas Mark 5) in very high sponge tins as this cake rises high.

BLUE PETER (Britain)
BBC TV children's programme

Muesli Fingers

125 g (4 oz) honey or golden syrup (see note)
90 g (3 oz) brown sugar
125 g (4 oz) margarine
90 g (3 oz) wholemeal flour
250 g (8 oz) *basic* muesli, with fruit and nuts

Put honey or golden syrup into a saucepan, add the brown sugar and margarine. Melt slowly over a *low* heat. Don't let the mixture boil. Make sure every grain of sugar has melted before you take it off the heat.

Mix the wholemeal flour and muesli and then add to the liquid. Stir until thoroughly mixed up. You can also add some additional chopped nuts as an optional extra.

Line a Swiss roll tin with kitchen foil and grease well with margarine paper. Spread the mixture evenly all over the tin. Bake for 30 minutes until golden brown in a pre-heated oven at 180°C (350°F, Gas Mark 4).

Cut into fingers before it cools (watch out for your fingers — don't burn them!). Allow to cool slightly, but remove from tin whilst still warm.
Makes 20–24

Note: An easy method to weigh the golden syrup is to put your saucepan on the scales and add the syrup until it weighs an extra 125 g (4 oz).

RABBI LIONEL BLUE (Britain), From *Kitchen Blues*
Radio and TV personality, cookery writer

Macho Beef Olives

Men are partial to meat and mustard. Here is a 'macho' dish for hungry carnivorous males. They will be very happy with it because they can bang about, and tie knots, and hit things.

3–4 kg (1½–2 lb) beef (4 slices from near rump)
2 tablespoons French mustard
2 tablespoons raw easy-cook rice
1 hard-boiled egg
2 pickled gherkins
1 large onion
1 clove garlic, crushed
300 ml (½ pint) light ale
30 g (1 oz) margarine
pinch sugar
1 bay-leaf
salt and pepper

Ask your butcher to cut you four slices of meat for beef olives. He will probably cut them near the rump. With a meat tenderiser such as a mallet or rolling-pin, beat the slices until they are very thin (this will be good for your aggression). Cut each of them across into two.

Spread each slice with French mustard. At the thin end put a ½ tablespoon of raw easy-cook rice, quarter of a hard-boiled egg and half a pickled gherkin cut lengthwise. Roll up the slices and secure them with string.

Cut the onion into rings and fry the rings in margarine with a pinch of sugar until dark brown. Lay the olives on top and sweat them for a few minutes. Add the garlic to the pan and enough simmering light ale to cover the olives but only just. Add a bay-leaf, season with more salt and pepper, and cook slowly covered for about 1½ hours. Untie the string or cut it, lay the olives on a serving dish, remove the bay-leaf and liquidise the gravy. Pour the gravy over the olives.

If the cooking pan doesn't look too dreadful (you are all men together), then don't bother to liquidise, munch the bay-leaf, and serve straight from the pan.

All it needs is mashed potatoes or rice to accompany it.

Where are the olives? That's what you've made!

Serves 4–6

ALAN BOND (Australia)
Entrepreneur

Minestrone

2 tablespoons olive or sunflower oil
250 g (8 oz) onions, finely chopped
125 g (4 oz) carrots, thinly sliced, quartered if large
125 g (4 oz) celery, sliced
250 g (8 oz) potatoes, diced
250 g (8 oz) tomatoes, skinned
250 g (8 oz) green or white cabbage, coarsely chopped
125 g (4 oz) shelled fresh or frozen peas
125 g (4 oz) green beans, cut into short lengths
125 g (4 oz) soya beans, cooked
200 ml (⅓ pint) dry red wine
2 litres (3⅓ pints) hot water
2 teaspoons yeast extract
4 cloves garlic, peeled and finely chopped
125 g (4 oz) stellette, or spaghetti broken into very short pieces
salt
freshly ground pepper
125 g (4 oz) Parmesan cheese, freshly grated

Heat the oil in a large pan and fry the onions, carrots and celery until the vegetables are golden brown, stirring well so that they cook evenly. Add the rest of the ingredients except the salt, pepper and Parmesan and bring the soup to the boil. Lower the heat and let it simmer for 20–30 minutes, adding a little extra water if necessary, then season with salt and pepper. Serve with chunks of freshly made wholemeal bread and hand a bowl of Parmesan separately.

For a change, serve with Pesto, also handed separately.

Serves 6

SIR DONALD BRADMAN (Australia)
Legendary Test cricketer

Devilled Steak

rump or fillet steak

Sauce
2 tablespoons (1½ oz) sugar
2 teaspoons dark jam (preferably plum)
2 tablespoons tomato sauce
3 teaspoons Worcestershire sauce
2 tablespoons vinegar
pinch salt

    Mix all sauce ingredients together in bottom of griller tray. Marinate steak in the sauce for 2 hours, turning several times. When ready to cook, lift steak on to top of griller leaving sauce in the lower part. Grill for 10 minutes. Serve lower juice as gravy.

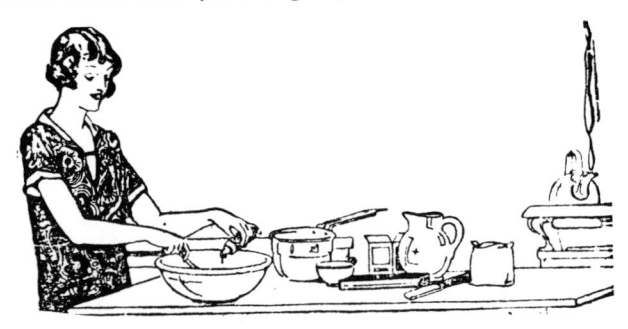

BROWN BROTHERS MILAWA VINEYARD (Australia)
From their Wine and Food Book

Hors-d'oeuvres

Caviare Profiteroles

This savoury is based on tiny choux pastry puffs filled with egg and topped with caviare. Half the filling can be made and the remaining puffs frozen for another time. Before using thaw puffs for about 4–5 minutes in moderate oven 200°C (400°F, Gas Mark 6).

Choux Pastry
½ cup cold water
60 g (3 oz) butter, cut into small pieces
½ cup (2 oz) flour
¼ teaspoon salt
2 large eggs

Place cold water in saucepan, add butter, bring to boil making certain butter is melted when water boils. Sift flour and salt on to piece of paper. Remove pan from heat, add all flour. Stir well, return to heat. Cook until it leaves sides of pan and begins to film base of pan, which usually takes a minute. Cool for 2 minutes.

Beat eggs with fork, gradually add to pastry, beating well. This can be done by hand, or by using a mixer or processor. Beaten well with a wooden spoon, ingredients should mix well in a few minutes. All the egg may not be needed — mixture should hold a shape when lifted with spoon.

Grease baking tray with butter. Put mixture into pastry bag with large plain tube, pipe out small portions about 2.5 cm (1 inch) in diameter, or place teaspoonsful of mixture on to tray. Use egg mixed with teaspoon of milk to glaze tops of puffs.

Bake puffs in moderate oven 200°C (400°F, Gas Mark 6) for about 20 minutes, reduce heat to 180°C (350°F, Gas Mark 4) and leave for further 5–10 minutes. When cooked and crisp remove from tray, pierce side of each one to release steam, otherwise they will soften. Turn oven off, leave door open, allow puffs to dry and cool for 10 minutes.

Puffs can be kept in airtight tin for up to a week. If they do soften, place in oven for a few minutes and they will become crisp again.

Filling
6 hard-boiled eggs
salt and pepper
1 tablespoon finely grated white onion
2 tablespoons well-flavoured mayonnaise
3 teaspoons finely chopped parsley
sour cream for topping
1 x 45 g (1½ oz) jar each red and black caviare (smoked salmon can be used to replace or alternate with caviare)

Mash hard-boiled eggs with salt, pepper, onion, mayonnaise and parsley. Mixture should be moist and well seasoned. Cut top from each choux puff; using a teaspoon or coffee spoon fill each with egg mixture, mounding slightly. Place dob of sour cream on top, then some caviare of each colour. Puffs can be filled about 30 minutes before serving, but no sooner or they will soften.

Makes 30 savouries

Note: Ideally the caviare is added almost at the last moment, especially if using black caviare, as colouring makes the sour cream a grey colour.

Marinated Scallops in Bacon

500 g (1 lb) scallops
15 slices bacon

Marinade
¼ cup oil
1 tablespoon soy sauce
2 cloves garlic, crushed
juice 1 lemon
ground pepper
dill

Place scallops in bowl with marinade, allow to stand approximately 2 hours. Stir occasionally. Drain scallops, wrap in ½ slice bacon and secure with a toothpick. Place under griller, turn once until bacon is crisp.
Quantity depends on scallop size

MAX BYGRAVES (Britain)
Entertainer

Stilton Soup

Often one is at a loose end wondering what to do with old Stilton (after all, it is pretty expensive). Never discard it — just keep any remaining pieces wrapped and in the deep-freeze until such times that you might need an unusual chilled soup on a hot summer evening or for a special dinner party.

300 ml (½ pint) thickened (double) cream
600 ml (1 pint) milk
90 g (3 oz) Stilton, preferably stale, finely grated
1 spring onion, finely chopped
3–4 walnuts, roughly chopped
1 eating apple
sprig parsley

Pour the cream into a mixer, whip slowly until it peaks. Slowly add the milk, cheese and spring onion alternately, taking care not to over-speed. When the liquid is at a creamy consistency, carefully remove and transfer to a sizeable soup tureen.

Chill in the fridge until 30 minutes before you are ready to serve it. Add the roughly chopped walnuts and the peeled and diced apple (but do not cut the apple beforehand otherwise it will discolour). Return the tureen to the fridge, chill until required.

Serve in individual soup cups or plates. Before serving, top with parsley to add colour.

Serves 4–6

The Bygraves Special

A delicious dessert. Always a family favourite. Incidentally, it lends itself to various fruits and similar-flavoured jelly.

600 ml (1 pint) thickened (double) cream
1 large tin crushed pineapple
1 packet pineapple jelly, made and cut into squares

Strain all the juice from the pineapple. Pour the pineapple juice into a saucepan, making the amount up to 600 ml (1 pint) with added water. Bring to the boil. Place the jelly squares into a jug, pour the hot liquid over them and stir until dissolved. Allow to cool but not set.

Pour the cream into a mixer, whip until it peaks. Remove very carefully into a crystal serving bowl. Slowly fold into the cream the crushed pineapple. Gently pour over it the very cool jelly. You will notice that the cream will rise in attractive shapes. Allow to set in the fridge no less than ½ hour.

Serves 4–6

ROBERT CARRIER (Britain)
Cookery expert

Chinese Pepper Steak with Rice

750 g (1½ lb) sirloin steak, 25 mm (1 inch) thick
375 g (12 oz) long-grain rice
100 ml (3 fl. oz) vegetable oil
1 large garlic clove, finely chopped
large pinch salt
¾ teaspoon ground ginger
¾ teaspoon crushed black peppercorns
2 green peppers, seeded and thinly sliced
1½ Spanish onions, thinly sliced
45–60 ml (1½–2 fl. oz) soy sauce
1½ teaspoons soft dark brown sugar
½ cup light beef stock
125 g (4 oz) canned water chestnuts, drained and sliced
4 spring onions, cut into 12 mm (½ inch) pieces

Steam the rice. Select a round heatproof dish in which the rice will lie 25 mm (1 inch) deep. Place the dish on a trivet standing in a large heavy-based saucepan. Cover the rice with 25 mm (1 inch) boiling water.

Pour boiling water into the bottom of the pan to come up to the base of the dish. Bring back to the boil, cover tightly and steam the rice over low heat for 30 minutes, without removing the lid. Transfer to a serving dish and keep warm.

Meanwhile, cut the steak downwards into 3 mm (⅛ inch) strips.

Heat the oil in a wok or large frying-pan. Add the garlic, salt, ginger and peppercorns and cook for 1–2 minutes, stirring with a wooden spoon. Add the steak strips and stir-fry over a high heat for 3–4 minutes, or until the strips are golden brown, tossing with a spatula. Remove from the pan with a slotted spoon and keep warm.

Add the peppers and onions to the spiced oil. Stir-fry for 4 minutes or until lightly coloured, tossing with a spatula. Return the steak strips to the pan. Add the soy sauce, sugar, beef stock and water chestnuts. Simmer for 1 minute and correct the seasoning if necessary.

Transfer the mixture to a heated serving dish and garnish with spring onion segments. Serve immediately with the steamed rice.

Serves 4

Biscuit Tortoni

2 large egg whites
pinch salt
¼ cup (2 oz) castor sugar
300 ml (½ pint) thickened (double) cream
125 g (4 oz) blanched almonds, coarsely chopped and toasted
¼ cup brandy, Marsala or medium-dry sherry

If using the freezing compartment of the refrigerator, about 1 hour before preparing ice-cream mixture turn refrigerator down to its lowest temperature (highest setting). Then chill a 1.2 litre (2 pint) loaf tin or a similarly sized pate mould.

Place the egg whites in a large, clean, dry mixing bowl and add a pinch of salt. Whisk the egg whites until they will stand in soft peaks. Then whisk in the castor sugar in four batches. When all the sugar has been incorporated, continue whisking until the meringue is stiff and glossy.

Without bothering to wash the whisk, whisk the cream until it will just hold its shape. Using a spatula or a large metal spoon, lightly but thoroughly fold the whipped cream into the meringue together with half the toasted almonds. Then fold in the brandy, Marsala or sherry.

Turn the cream mixture into the chilled container and smooth the surface. Cover the container with kitchen foil and place in the freezing compartment of the refrigerator for 3–4 hours or until the ice-cream is very firm.

Thirty minutes before serving, dip the loaf tin or pate mould in hot water for 2–3 seconds to loosen the ice-cream. Invert a serving dish on top of the container, then sharply invert both plate and container. Gently lift off the container to unmould the ice-cream. Sprinkle the reserved almonds over the top and sides of the ice-cream, then place in the main body of the refrigerator until serving time. To serve, cut the tortoni into thick, even-sized slices.
Serves 4

PAT CASH (Australia)
Tennis player

Bran Muffins

My health muffins for snacks.

1 cup bran
1 cup skim milk
1 egg
30 g (1 oz) margarine
1 cup (5 oz) raisins
1 cup (5 oz) chopped dates
1 cup (4 oz) chopped pecans

1 cup (4 oz) chopped walnuts
1 cup (4 oz) plain flour
1½ teaspoons baking powder
1 teaspoon honey
1 teaspoon cinnamon
½ teaspoon nutmeg

Combine bran and milk. Add egg and melted margarine and beat well. Mix in fruit and nuts.

Combine flour, baking powder, honey, cinnamon and nutmeg. Stir in with mixture only until combined.

Fill muffin tins and bake in a pre-heated oven 200°C (400°F, Gas Mark 6) for 20–25 minutes.

Makes 12

Fish in Lemon Butter

A quick way to make tasty fish.

60 g (2 oz) butter or margarine
¼ cup (1 oz) plain flour
¼ cup lemon juice
1 kg (2 lb) fish fillets

1 teaspoon chopped fresh parsley
1 cup chopped celery
pepper to taste

Place butter in shallow glass casserole dish and melt. Blend in flour, lemon juice, parsley, celery, pepper.

Arrange fillets in sauce. Cover with plastic wrap and cook on high in a microwave for 14–15 minutes.

CHARLES, HRH THE PRINCE OF WALES

Leek and Noodle Casserole

350 g (11 oz) wholemeal noodles
oil
4–5 leeks
granulated vegetable stock
curry powder
grated cheese
(single) cream

Boil the noodles in salted water (with a little oil) until soft, then drain.

Cut the leeks into 1.5 cm (½ inch) pieces, wash, and then saute in a large pan with some oil and water. Add a small amount of granulated vegetable stock and curry powder to give a very mild taste, cook until soft but not coloured.

Place in a casserole dish in alternate layers of leeks and noodles. As a fifth layer, cover with grated cheese and pour over this some cream. Bake in a hot oven until crisp and golden — approximately 20 minutes.

DIANE CILENTO (Australia)
Actor

Tongues a la Tony

As Kurt Weill said:
First feed the face and then talk right and wrong,
For even honest folk can act like sinners
Unless they have their customary dinners.
I believe him to be correct.

2 fresh, smoked or salted beef tongues
onions, bay-leaf, peppercorns
1–2 tablespoons treacle or golden syrup

If salted tongues, soak them in water to remove salt; or put them in saucepan, bring to boil, throw out water, and repeat process. Rinse in cold water. Leave skin on.

Place tongues in saucepan of water (to top) with quartered onions, bay-leaf, peppercorns, treacle or golden syrup, and simmer slowly over low heat 2½–3 hours until done and tender. Remove and discard vegetables.

Cook some vegetables, including carrots, to serve with meat, and add one of the following sauces. Tongue is also delicious served cold.

To skin tongues
Cut incision on underside of the tongues and pull back skin, which should come off easily, starting at the tip and working back. Cut off and remove membranes, etc., underneath.

To carve
Slice it across.

To serve
Lay slices of tongue on plate, and surround it with cooled vegetables and/or boiled potatoes.

Piquant Tomato Sauce

Simmer skinned fresh tomatoes with 1–2 cloves garlic and 1–2 tablespoons sugar. Puree or mash. Add chilli if trying to appease a palate for hot things.

Caper or Mustard Sauce

To basic white sauce add either chopped capers or prepared mustard.

Lemon Delicious

9 eggs
300 g (10 oz) sugar
900 ml (1½ pints) milk
¼ cup (1 oz) self-raising flour
pinch salt
grated rind and juice of 6 lemons

Beat egg yolks and half the sugar together until thick and light. Gradually beat in milk, flour, salt, lemon rind and juice.
Beat egg whites until stiff. Add rest of sugar and continue beating for 1 minute. Fold egg whites into the lemon mixture. Spoon into a greased baking dish and place in pan of hot water. Bake in pre-heated moderate oven 160°C (325°F, Gas Mark 3) for 1 hour or until soft.
Serves 12

COUNTRY LIVING Magazine (Britain)
Philippa Davenport, cookery writer

Chrysanthemum Duck

With its glorious glaze and the bitter-sweet fragrance of the accompanying salad, this makes a sensational alternative to classic crispy roast duck. No problems about carving — duck joints are used. Just add or subtract to cater for larger or smaller parties.

6 large duck joints
fresh root ginger
5 small thin-skinned oranges
2 tablespoons runny honey
2 teaspoons soy sauce
1–2 large chrysanthemums, preferably tawny gold
watercress or chicory
a few unsalted cashew nuts, toasted under the grill

Remove any lumps of excess fat from the duck joints and prick the skin all over with a fork, angling it carefully to avoid piercing deep into the flesh or precious meat juices as well as fat will run out during cooking.

Peel and chop very finely indeed 2 generous tablespoons fresh root ginger. Lay the duck joints in a dish and rub them all over with the ginger and a good grinding of pepper, but no salt. Pour on 2 tablespoons juice freshly squeezed from one orange. Turn the meat several times to moisten it all over. Cover and set aside in a cool place for several hours, preferably overnight, so the duck absorbs some of the flavours.

Drain the marinade from the duck and scrape off the ginger. Reserve this and the marinade liquid. Put the duck joints, skin side up, on to a rack in a baking dish or roasting tin and roast in an oven heated to 200°C (400°F, Gas Mark 6) for 45 minutes. (If the duck joints are very large and your oven is quite small you may need to use two dishes and two racks — and swap oven positions half-way through cooking.)

Stand the honey jar in a bowl of hot water for 10 minutes so that the honey becomes runny enough to measure easily. Mix honey with the orange and ginger marinade mixture then stir in the soy sauce plus a pinch of salt to make an aromatic glaze. Pour off the duck fat that has collected in the roasting tin — save it for frying. Brush the glaze all over the flesh and skin of the duck and continue roasting, still with skin side up and still on the rack, for another 20 minutes. Baste once during this time, making sure that all the little pieces of ginger adhere to the duck skin. By the end of cooking time the meat should be well cooked yet succulent and the skin should be burnished to a rich mahogany-coloured glaze. If the duck looks in danger of burning cover the dish with a dome of foil. More probably it will be necessary to cover only the wing tips or drumsticks — the parts which are most prone to burning.

To make the accompanying salad, first peel 3–4 of the oranges. Use a very sharp knife and be ruthless about cutting away every trace of the bitter white pith. Slice the oranges across into thin rounds, sprinkle them with a little pepper, a scrunch of sea salt and a drizzle of oil. Arrange them prettily in a shallow dish. Add a few nuts if you wish and a scant handful of chicory leaves or watercress sprigs, but bear in mind that the salad should be composed mainly of orange and chrysanthemum. Immediately before serving, sprinkle the salad with another spoonful of oil and a squeeze of orange, then quickly pile the fresh chrysanthemum petals on top. The slightly bitter fragrance of the flowers complements the rich glazed duck beautifully. Huge tawny gold blooms look most dramatic: simply pull the petals from the flower-heads, tugging them gently, a small handful at a time, so they do not become bruised or spoiled.

Serves 6

Hot Raspberry and Redcurrant Tarts

Cooking raspberries just long enough to make them warm heightens their fragrance beautifully and these tarts make a lovely choice of pudding for a cool day. They are surprisingly filling. The finishing touches and final cooking must be done immediately before serving, so this recipe is better suited to relaxed and informal occasions than to grand entertaining. Although you could use a mixture of white and wholemeal flour, and you could use a butter substitute, I think white flour and butter are best for the orange-flavoured pastry used here.

155 g (5 oz) butter
2½ cups (10 oz) plain flour
finely grated zest of a small orange
2½ tablespoons freshly squeezed orange juice
500 g (1 lb) raspberries
250 g (½ lb) redcurrants
90 g (3 oz) vanilla sugar

Cut then rub the butter into the sifted flour. Stir in the orange zest and bind the dough with the orange juice. Knead the pastry lightly, roll it out and use it to line six 11 cm (4–4½ inch) individual fluted tart tins with removable bases. Line the pastry shells with greaseproof paper and weigh down with baking beans. Blind bake on a pre-heated baking sheet for 15 minutes at 200°C (400°F, Gas Mark 6). Remove lining paper and beans and bake the pastry for a further 15 minutes until pale golden and crisp. Cool the tarts completely before wrapping and storing them in an airtight tin. (Keep the tarts in their tins to protect the pastry against breakage.)

Shortly before serving, unwrap the tarts and slide them out of their tins on to a baking sheet. Put the baking sheet into an oven heated to 180°C (350°F, Gas Mark 4) and leave for 10 minutes or so until the pastry is hot. Sprinkle the raspberries and redcurrants with the vanilla sugar and toss gently to mix. Pile the fruit into the pastry shells and cook for 7–8 minutes only. The idea is to make the fruit warm and aromatic, not to cook it until squashy and flowing with juices. Use a fish slice to transfer the tarts to very hot pudding plates and serve immediately — with softly whipped cream, *fromage blanc*, or yoghurt if you wish.

Serves 6

THE COUNTRY WOMEN'S ASSOCIATION OF VICTORIA INC. (Australia)

Rabbit Venison

The early settlers in Australia imported the rabbit from England, as game, back in the nineteenth century.

In this wide open country, so different from the woods and copses in England, these prolific breeders soon grew to plague proportions, eating out the pastures on the farms. Poisoning was tried, but it was not until the disease myxomatosis was introduced, spread by means of the mosquito and later by the rabbit flea, that the rabbit population was able to be controlled.

This was a post World War Two development, but during the great depression between the wars the rabbit became a staple form of diet, particularly for people in the country, and in many cases was used as a substitute for chicken.

Rabbits were hunted or trapped and skins sold to be used in fabrics, fur felt or even in the so-called Lapin fur coats — the poor man's fur. Housewives devised many ways of serving the humble rabbit to relieve the monotony of the diet. The meat is very low in fat.

This recipe is one of the recipes used, but roast rabbit, pan-fried rabbit, rabbit fricassee, rabbit pate, are simply a few of the ways of serving the rabbit.

1 rabbit	1 teaspoon sage or mixed herbs
seasoned plain flour	1 onion
3 rashers bacon	1 cup stock
1 cup (2 oz) soft white breadcrumbs	30 g (1 oz) butter

Wash and joint the rabbit, dip joints in seasoned flour and place half of them in a greased casserole. Cut bacon into small strips and lay in casserole. Add the remainder of rabbit, breadcrumbs mixed with sage or herbs, chopped onion and stock.

Cover casserole and cook in moderately slow oven for 2½ hours. Remove lid, dot with butter, and return to oven for 30 minutes.

NICOLA COX © (Britain)
Cookery writer and demonstrator

Soupe de Poisson

100 ml (3 fl. oz) olive oil
2 medium onions
1 leek
1 stick celery
3 cloves garlic
1 kg (2 lb) tomatoes, skinned and chopped
thyme, parsley, fennel
1 bay-leaf
strip lemon peel
150 ml (¼ pint) dry white wine
salt, pepper
1 packet or a good pinch saffron, soaked in hot water 15–30 minutes
pinch mace
1 litre (1¾ pints) water
250 g (½ lb) smoked cod or haddock
500 g (1 lb) mussels in their shells, well-scrubbed
   OR 125 g (¼ lb) frozen shell-less mussels (optional)
250 g (½ lb) jewfish (halibut) or cod
125 g (¼ lb) shelled prawns (optional)
several well-washed scallops (black thread removed and cut up) (optional)

To finish
finely chopped parsley
grated lemon rind

Cover the bottom of a large pan with good olive oil and heat gently. Add the finely sliced onions, leek and diced celery and fry gently until beginning to brown, taking 15–20 minutes. Add the chopped garlic, tomatoes and a little thyme, parsley, fresh fennel (or fennel seeds), bay-leaf and lemon peel. Cook 4–5 minutes before adding the wine, a very little salt and pepper, the soaked saffron, a pinch of mace and the water. Simmer briskly for 20–30 minutes.

Skin and bone the fish and cut into large cubes. Add first the smoked fish and fresh mussels (if used); four minutes later the fresh white fish; and finally, three minutes later, the prawns, scallops and frozen mussels, which need only 3–5 minutes. Sprinkle with chopped parsley and grated lemon rind before serving with hot French bread.

Serves 6–8

Coupe Juli

some cauliflower florets
1–2 avocado pears (depending on size)
2 pears or ¼ small melon
10 cm (4 inch) cucumber

Toss the cauliflower florets into boiling salt water for 2 minutes to blanch, then refresh in cold water until chilled; drain well.

Dressing
½ teaspoon honey
½ teaspoon Dijon mustard
30 ml (1 fl. oz) lemon juice
salt and pepper
90 ml (3 fl. oz) olive oil
1 tablespoon each of fresh finely chopped chives, parsley, mint

Mix together the honey, mustard, lemon juice, salt and pepper, then gradually beat in the oil to make a dressing. Stir in the herbs. Peel and dice the avocado, pears (or melon) and cucumber and turn into the dressing with the cauliflower. Mix thoroughly and leave to chill for 2–4 hours, mixing once or twice.

Serve well chilled in individual glasses, accompanied by brown bread spread with anchovy butter and rolled up.
Serves 4–6

CRANKS HEALTH FOODS (Britain)
Restaurants and shops

Armenian Soup

This recipe was introduced to Cranks by an Australian member of staff many years ago and has become a great favourite in our restaurant.

60 g (2 oz) red lentils, washed
60 g (2 oz) dried apricots, washed
1 large potato
1.2 litres (2 pints) vegetable stock
juice of ½ lemon
1 teaspoon ground cumin
3 tablespoons chopped parsley
salt and pepper to taste

Place lentils and apricots in a large saucepan. Roughly chop the potato and add to the pan with remaining ingredients. Bring to the boil, cover and simmer for 30 minutes. Allow to cool, then blend in a liquidiser until smooth. Reheat to serving temperature and adjust seasoning to taste.
Serves 4–6

White Cabbage and Orange Salad

A simple, colourful and nutritious salad — serve it as a starter.

375 g (12 oz) white cabbage
3 oranges
60 g (2 oz) sunflower seeds
¼ cup chopped parsley
150 ml (¼ pint) natural yoghurt
salt and pepper to taste

Finely shred the cabbage. Peel the oranges, remove all the white pith, then cut the orange segments away from the membrane. Combine the cabbage, orange segments and remaining ingredients. Toss well.
Serves 6

Creamy Leek Croustade

The delightful contrast in flavours and textures of this layered savoury makes it ideal for a dinner party.

Base
3 cups (6 oz) fresh wholemeal breadcrumbs
60 g (2 oz) butter or margarine
125 g (4 oz) cheddar cheese, grated
125 g (4 oz) mixed nuts, chopped
½ teaspoon mixed herbs
1 clove garlic, crushed

Sauce
3 medium-sized leeks
4 tomatoes
60 g (2 oz) butter or margarine
30 g (1 oz) 100% wholemeal flour
300 ml (½ pint) milk
salt and pepper to taste
¼ cup (½ oz) fresh wholemeal breadcrumbs

To make the base, put the breadcrumbs in a basin, rub in the butter, then add the remaining ingredients. Press the mixture into a 28 x 18 cm (11 x 7 inch) tin. Bake in the oven at 220°C (425°F, Gas Mark 7) for 15–20 minutes, until golden brown.

Meanwhile, slice the leeks and chop the tomatoes. Melt the butter in a saucepan. Saute the leeks for 5 minutes, then stir in the flour. Add the milk, stirring constantly, then bring to the boil, reduce heat to a simmer. Add the remaining ingredients, except breadcrumbs, and simmer for a few minutes to soften the tomatoes. Check seasoning. Spoon the vegetable mixture over the base, sprinkle with breadcrumbs and heat through in the oven at 180°C (350°F, Gas Mark 4) for 20 minutes. Serve at once.

Serves 6

Millet and Peanut Cookies

A well-tried favourite and very popular at Cranks.

¼ cup oil
¼ teaspoon salt
1 free-range egg
⅓ cup (3 oz) raw brown sugar
125 g (4 oz) peanuts, ground
90 g (3 oz) raisins
125 g (4 oz) millet flakes

Lightly whisk together the oil, salt, egg and sugar. Stir in the remaining ingredients until well blended. Roll the mixture into 10 balls. Place on a lightly greased baking sheet. Press each one down to flatten slightly. Bake in the oven at 180°C (350°F, Gas Mark 4) for about 15 minutes, until golden. Allow to cool on the baking sheet for a few minutes before transferring to a wire tray.
Makes 10

HECTOR CRAWFORD (Australia)
Film Producer

Iced Prawn Cream Soup

500 g (1 lb) green prawns
500 ml (16 fl. oz) milk
1 tablespoon cornflour
1 tablespoon butter

salt and pepper
1 tablespoon vinegar
125 ml (4 fl. oz) cream

Shell prawns. Reserve heads and shells, simmer them with half the milk for 1 hour. Strain, add remaining milk and prawns — keeping larger ones for decoration. Simmer for 15 minutes.

Blend cornflour to a smooth paste with a little cold milk. Add to milk mixture, season, simmer 3–4 minutes. Remove from heat, add butter, seasoning and vinegar, stir until melted, then cool. Add cream and chill.

A few drops of red colouring may be added for pink prawn look. Garnish with prawns.

Prawn Kebabs

Cooked on the barbecue over hot coals.

500 g (1 lb) green prawns	2 cloves garlic
¼ cup olive oil	1 teaspoon salt
¼ cup dry sherry	freshly ground pepper
1 teaspoon green ginger, finely chopped	4 shallots, finely chopped

Devein prawns. Rinse in cold water, drain on paper towels. Mix together remaining ingredients. Marinate prawns in this mixture for at least 1 hour. Thread prawns on skewers. Place over hot coals and baste with marinade until lightly browned and cooked.

The prawns may be served as a first course. As a main course serve with rice, French salad and lemon wedges.

Wagga Wagga Beer Chops

12 lean lamb chops	1 can tomato soup
seasoned flour	sugar
butter	beer
2 large onions	

Trim all fat off chops. Roll in seasoned flour, brown lightly in butter, place in ovenproof dish. Peel, slice and lightly brown onions, put in with chops. Add tomato soup and sprinkle with sugar. Add sufficient beer to cover chops (as if using water). Extra salt and pepper may be needed. Cook in a moderate oven approximately 1½ hours.

JOSCELINE DIMBLEBY (Britain), From *Main Attractions*
Cookery writer

Beef and Mushroom Pie with Cheesy Suet Crust

Pies look beautiful and everyone seems to like them. This is a tasty pie with a double cheesy crust.

Filling
500 g (1 lb) minced beef
salt and black pepper
a little cooking fat or oil
1–2 cloves garlic, chopped finely
3 teaspoons tomato puree
1–2 teaspoons paprika
125 g (4 oz) mushrooms

Crust
1½ cups (6 oz) plain flour
1 teaspoon baking powder
¼ teaspoon salt
1 cup (2 oz) fresh white breadcrumbs
60 g (2 oz) cheese, grated
125 g (4 oz) shredded suet

   Season the mince with salt and black pepper. Melt a little fat in a pan and fry the mince for about 3–4 minutes over a strong heat, stirring with a wooden spoon. Add the garlic, tomato puree and paprika. Remove from the heat and stir in the mushrooms. Check for seasoning and let the mixture cool.
   To make the pastry, sift the flour, baking powder and salt into a bowl and stir in the breadcrumbs, cheese and suet. Add enough cold water to form a stiff dough.
   Pre-heat the oven to 200°C (400°F, Gas Mark 6). Grease a 23–25 cm (9–10 inch) flat pie plate. Divide the pastry in half and roll on a floured board. Shape into two circles big enough for the pie plate. Line the plate with one circle and spoon in the meat filling. Dampen the edges and cover with the other circle. Trim the edges and roll out the trimmings to cut out decorations for the top. Brush with milk and bake in the centre of the oven for 25–30 minutes, until golden brown.
   A green vegetable or green salad is all that is needed to accompany this pie.
Serves 4–6

KEN DONE (Australia)
Artist

Grilled Crayfish Tails with Basil Butter

I always love very simple seafood — prawns, oysters, lobster, grilled fish, etc. — accompanied by a salad. One of my favourite salads is fresh Italian Bocconchini and tomato, both sliced, with plenty of fresh basil and sprinkled with olive oil.

crayfish tails
salt and pepper
olive oil

unsalted butter
plenty of fresh basil

Pre-heat the grill or barbecue. Halve the crayfish tails, season with salt and pepper and sprinkle with olive oil. Grill them for 5 minutes on the flesh side and 5 minutes on the shell side (reverse if you are using the barbecue).

Put the butter and basil in a small saucepan and let it melt over a low heat. Turn the tails flesh side up and sprinkle liberally with the butter and basil and cook for a further 10 minutes (or until *just* done), basting frequently with the butter.

Serve with a tossed green salad.

Khoshaf (Dried Fruit Salad)

A Middle Eastern dessert in which the fruits are not stewed but macerated.

500 g (1 lb) dried apricots
250 g (½ lb) prunes
125 g (¼ lb) raisins
125 g (¼ lb) blanched almonds
60 g (2 oz) pine-nuts

sugar
1 tablespoon rose-water
1 tablespoon orange blossom water
fresh pomegranate seeds

Wash the fruits if necessary, put them into a large bowl. Mix with the nuts and cover with water. Add sugar to taste and sprinkle with rose-water and orange blossom water. Let the fruits soak for at least 48 hours. The syrup becomes rich with the juices of the fruit and acquires a lovely golden colour.

If available use pomegranate seeds to make a delicious variation.

ED DOOLAN (Britain)
Radio WM Birmingham personality

Pavlova

8 egg whites
2 cups (14 oz) castor sugar
2 teaspoons cornflour
2 teaspoons brown vinegar

Beat egg whites until stiff. Add sugar gradually until dissolved completely — this is important. Mix in cornflour and vinegar together. Do not over-beat once these ingredients have been added.

Grease a large flat dish with oil and spoon mixture on to pan and spread with spatula to create a shell with the sides higher than the centre. Place in a pre-heated oven 180°C (350°F, Gas Mark 4) on the bottom rack, and immediately turn down to 140°C (275°F, Gas Mark 1). Bake in oven 1¼ hours. Do not open door during cooking.

To cool, open oven door and leave to cool in oven for 20–30 minutes. This will stop the shell cracking.

Note: This makes a very large shell and can be adjusted for a smaller Pavlova.

Filling
For an authentic Australian Pavlova, fill shell with whipped cream, strawberries, sliced banana and passionfruit pulp.

THE DORCHESTER (Britain)
Cuisinier Anton Mosimann

Terrine of Oranges with Raspberry Sauce

Pave d'oranges a la sauce framboise

To turn the terrine out of its dish once set, dip the base of the dish carefully into hot water then place a plate over the top and invert. You could use orange juice in this recipe instead of apple juice for a more concentrated orange flavour.

18 medium oranges
8 leaves gelatine, soaked in cold water and squeezed dry
600 ml (1 pint) clear apple juice
1 bunch fresh mint leaves
8 teaspoons Grenadine syrup
½ cup water
15 tiny mint sprigs for garnish
fresh raspberries for garnish

Raspberry Sauce
500 g (1 lb) raspberries
45 g (1½ oz) icing sugar
3 teaspoons lemon juice

Pare the rind from three washed oranges and cut into thin julienne strips. Reserve. Squeeze the juice from these oranges.

Cut away the peel and white pith from all the remaining oranges, and carefully remove the orange segments. Remove pips. Reserve the juice from the segmenting, add it to the other quantity, and strain it through a fine sieve.

Dissolve the gelatine in a little warm apple juice then add to the remaining apple juice. Add ½ cup of the strained orange juice to the apple juice.

Chill a 1.5 litre (2½ pint) china or glass terrine dish and spoon about 6 mm (¼ inch) juice over the base. Chill until set, then overlap some mint leaves to cover the jelly entirely.

Place the terrine in a large bowl of ice. Spoon a little jellied apple juice over each side in turn and press mint leaves on to each side. Chill until firm between each application.

Arrange half the orange segments on top of the mint leaves and spoon half the remaining juice over. Chill until set.

Arrange the remaining half of the orange segments on top and spoon the remaining juice over. Chill until set.

Place the orange rind julienne in a saucepan with the Grenadine syrup and water and simmer gently until almost all the liquid has evaporated and the orange strips have turned pink. Leave to cool. Add a little extra water if they become too syrupy.

To make the sauce, puree the fresh raspberries then strain through a sieve. Stir in the sugar and lemon juice.

To serve, carefully turn the terrine out of the dish, and very carefully slice. Spoon a little of the raspberry sauce on to each plate and centre a slice of the terrine on top. Decorate with orange julienne, a spring of mint, and a raspberry.

Serves 15

ELIZABETH DURACK CMG, OBE (Australia)
Illustrator

Poisson Alfresco

Some meals can be enjoyed with the very minimum of preparation or condiment — one such lingers in my memory when, years ago, with our father, my sister Mary and I were driving along the old bush road between Argyle and Ivanhoe Stations in the far north of Western Australia. On reaching the Ord River we negotiated the narrow cement causeway that served as a crossing in the dry season. Here a number of natives were spearing fish where the water cascaded over the rocks. One of them came forward and presented us with two beautiful gleaming bream. Being midday we decided to eat them then and there. Here then is the recipe for a wonderful repast.

a beautiful warm day
freshly caught fish
a shovel smeared with dripping
a dash of hunger sauce

Place fish on shovel over a low fire of river gum branches. Cook slowly, do not turn. Serve on a selected leaf from *Ficus leucotricha*.

MARY DURACK (Australia)
Author

Savoury Vegetable Casserole

1 white onion	2 tablespoons olive oil
1 zucchini	2 tomatoes
½ green capsicum	pinch oregano
½ red capsicum	salt and pepper
1 carrot	1 cup (6 oz) rice

Chop onion, zucchini and capsicum; thinly slice carrot. Saute in olive oil, stirring gently. Add tomatoes, oregano, salt and pepper. Put lid on the pot and cook gently for 4 minutes, stirring occasionally.

Cook rice and place in greased casserole, add cooked vegetables. Top with breadcrumbs and grated cheese. Place lid on casserole and cook gently in oven for 15–20 minutes.

Chicken with Orange Sauce

breast of chicken (as required)	2 tablespoons honey
seasoned flour	1 tablespoon Grand Marnier
juice of 2 oranges	

Remove skin from chicken and roll in seasoned flour. Cook gently in oil and remove from pan when lightly browned. Add a little flour to the pan and brown gently. Mix in orange juice, honey and Grand Marnier to make a sauce. Pour the sauce over the chicken breasts and serve.

JOHN ELEY, The Cooking Canon (Britain)
Radio and TV personality, cookery writer

Strawberry Ice-Cream

Enjoy this delicious recipe!!

250 g (8 oz) fresh strawberries
1¼ cups (7 oz) icing sugar
600 ml (1 pint) thickened (double) cream

In a food processor or liquidiser process the strawberries and icing sugar together to make a rich liquid. Blend in the cream.

Pour into a plastic freezer box and freeze for 40 minutes. Remove and beat with a wooden spoon. Keep repeating this process 2 or 3 times until you have a smooth ice-cream.

If you have an ice-cream maker then follow the manufacturer's instructions.

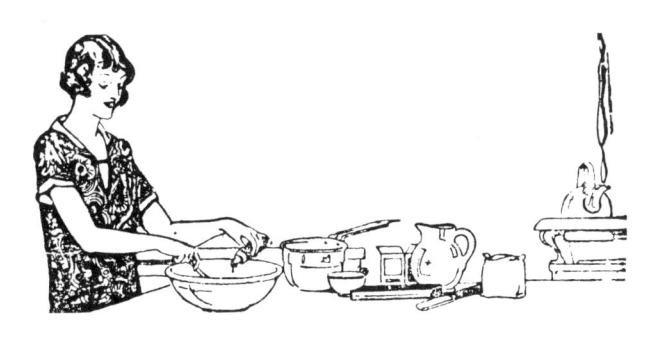

ETON COLLEGE (Britain)
From Poppy Anderson, Headmaster's wife

Lemon Up and Down Pudding

This has a sponge top and a lemon sauce base when cooked.

60 g (2 oz) margarine
½ cup (4 oz) castor sugar
1 lemon

1 large egg, separated
2 tablespoons plain flour
150 ml (¼ pint) milk

Cream margarine with castor sugar. Stir in the lemon rind and juice, egg yolk, flour and milk. Whip the egg white till stiff and fold in.

Pour the mixture into a greased pie dish and bake in a tray of cold water in a moderate oven 180°C (350°F, Gas Mark 4) for 1 hour.
Serves 3

KEITH FLOYD (Britain)
TV cooking personality

Spit Roast Leg of Lamb with Vegetables

1 boned leg of lamb
6 cloves garlic, peeled and sliced like thick almond flakes
1 small tin anchovy fillets
black pepper
oil
large bunch fresh rosemary twigs
1 tablespoon sea salt

Vegetable Garnish
8 potatoes, parboiled and cut into pieces 5 cm (2 inches) in diameter
8 carrots, parboiled and cut into pieces 5 cm x 2.5 cm (2 x 1 inch)
8 onions, parboiled and cut into pieces 5 cm (2 inches) in diameter
16 batons celery, parboiled and cut 5 cm (2 inches) long
16 cloves garlic, unpeeled

Make small incisions all over the leg and insert the slivers of garlic and strips of anchovy deep into the meat. Rub well with black pepper and thread on to the spit.

Place a drip tray under the spit and cook the lamb close to the fire for the first 15 minutes. Then lift higher and baste with oil, cooking for a further hour or so.

About 20 minutes before the end of the cooking process put all the parboiled vegetables and garlic cloves into the drip tray, which by now has collected fat from the joint — stir the vegetables around to coat them with fat and let them brown and get quite crunchy.

As the cooking process comes to an end and the fire is dying throw a handful of rosemary on to the fire, having first removed the drip tray, and let it burst into flames. Tip the vegetables and all the juices on to a serving dish, put the leg of lamb on top and leave just at the edge of the fire for 5–6 minutes to allow the lamb to 'settle'. Sprinkle the coarse ground sea salt over the lot, carve and serve.

Serves 4

MEM FOX (Australia)
Children's author

Anzac Biscuits

Anzac Biscuits were probably thought up in the First World War: ANZAC stands for Australian and New Zealand Army Corps. I adore Anzac Biscuits, so of course they're featured in Possum Magic.

1 cup (4 oz) flour	2 tablespoons butter
1 cup (7 oz) sugar	2 tablespoons golden syrup
1 cup (3 oz) desiccated coconut	1 teaspoon bicarbonate of soda
2 cups (6 oz) rolled oats	¼ cup boiling water

Mix dry ingredients together. Melt butter in syrup, add soda dissolved in water, add to dry ingredients. Combine well, roll into small balls and place on baking tray. Flatten with a fork. Cook in a moderate oven about 15 minutes until golden.

Pavlova

This is my English mother-in-law's favourite Australian food. It is a scrumptious meringue pudding/dessert calculated to make dinner guests want to be invited again and again!

4 egg whites	1 teaspoon vinegar
pinch salt	½ teaspoon vanilla
1¼ cups (8 oz) castor sugar	2 teaspoons cornflour

Topping
red jelly	fresh fruit

Beat egg whites with a pinch of salt for 5–6 minutes, gradually adding sugar, vinegar and vanilla. Beat till stiff. Sift in cornflour and fold in lightly.

Cover a 30 cm (12 inch) round tray with foil. Grease it lightly. Spoon the pavlova on to it and spread it evenly. In gas oven bake for 10 minutes at 200°C (400°F, Gas Mark 6) then at 110°C (225°F, Gas Mark ¼) for 1 hour. In electric oven pre-heat to 200°C (400°F) then set at 120°C (250°F) and bake undisturbed for 1½ hours.

Make up a red jelly. When set, chop up the jelly and place on base of cooled pavlova. Top with fresh fruit: bananas, peaches, kiwi-fruit or strawberries. Top with artistically piped whipped cream.
YUM!

THE RIGHT HONOURABLE MALCOLM FRASER CH
(Australia)
Former Prime Minister of Australia

> When Malcolm is overseas he thinks of home-grown food — turnips which have been grown in a back paddock for the cattle, made into an excellent ice-cold soup, followed by a rainbow trout caught in the dam. Tamie Fraser

Vegetable Soup

3 onions
6 turnips
2 potatoes
butter

chicken stock
seasonings
1 cup cream
chives

Chop the vegetables. Saute the onion in butter until clear, add turnips and potatoes. Cover with 1.5 cm (½ inch) of chicken stock (cubes may be used). Adjust seasoning, salt and pepper. Liquidise and chill.

Add 1 cup cream, serve sprinkled with chives.

Rainbow Trout

3 kg (6 lb) rainbow trout,
 caught in the dam
lemon juice

rosemary
butter
salt and pepper

Place trout on foil. Put inside some lemon juice, rosemary, butter, salt and pepper. Squeeze lemon juice over. Wrap foil. Bake at 180°C (350°F, Gas Mark 4) for 1 hour.

Serve with hot melted butter or hollandaise sauce.

TONY GREIG (Australia)
Cricketer

These recipes are Tony's real favourites — in fact, family favourites!
Tony's mother, Mrs Joyce Greig

Meringues

Being a Greig favourite, I double this recipe as these are the toffee and browny meringues, not the plain white ones.

1¼ cups (9 oz) sugar
2 level teaspoons baking powder

3 egg whites
2 teaspoons vanilla

Put half the sugar in a bowl and other half in another bowl. Add baking powder to one basin of sugar, mix and put on one side. Beat egg whites until stiff, gradually adding sugar *without* baking powder. When absolutely stiff *fold* in sugar with baking powder. Add vanilla. Bake in 150°C (300°F, Gas Mark 2) oven for 10 minutes, then turn oven down to 110°C (225°F, Gas Mark ¼) and leave for as long as you like. Store in airtight tin. Serve with ice-cream.

Seven-Cup Pudding

This recipe was sent to me by Tony's great-grandmother and has always been his favourite — even as a Christmas pudding.

1 teacupful breadcrumbs
1 teacupful flour
1 teacupful shredded suet
1 teacupful sugar
1 teacupful raisins

1 teacupful currants
1 teacupful milk
1 egg
½ teaspoon cinnamon
½ teaspoon bicarbonate of soda

Mix all dry ingredients. Beat egg and milk, mix with dry ingredients. Steam 2 hours and serve with sauce, cream or ice-cream. Deep-freezes well.

JO GRIFFITHS (Australia)
Cookery writer

Shrimps in Avocado Nest with Cherry Tomato Eggs

If quality shrimps are not available, substitute another cooked shellfish or fish cut into tiny bite-sized pieces — smoked fish is also delicious.

juice of 2 lemons
1½ teaspoons soy sauce
2 teaspoons sesame oil
200 g (7 oz) fresh or frozen shrimps (prawns)
2 large ripe avocados
salt and cayenne pepper
8 cherry tomatoes
lemon slices and fresh dill

Combine the juice of 1 lemon, soy sauce and sesame oil and mix well. Add the shrimps and stir until well coated.

Cut the avocados in half crosswise, as you would a lemon. Remove the seeds and peel. Cut a 1 cm (½ inch) thick medallion from the thickest part of each half, giving 4 slices. Brush with lemon juice.

Puree the remaining avocado in a food processor or push through a sieve. Add 1 teaspoon lemon juice, salt and cayenne pepper to taste. Using a star-shaped nozzle, pipe a border of avocado puree around the edge of the avocado disc. Reserve a little for garnish.

Fill the cavity with shrimps. Cut tops off cherry tomatoes and carefully remove seeds. Pipe avocado into the cavity.

Garnish with lemon and fresh dill.

Serves 4 as an entree

Mustard Seed Chicken with Spring Vegetables

A succulent, simple, one-dish meal ideal for lunch, dinner, or even a late night supper.

30 g (1 oz) butter
4 chicken fillets
1 carrot, peeled and cut into julienne strips
6 spring onions, cut into julienne strips
100 g (3½ oz) snow peas, topped, tailed and strings removed
1½ cups apple cider
½ cup cream
1 tablespoon seed mustard

Melt the butter in a large frying-pan over a medium heat and fry the chicken fillets for 5–6 minutes or until barely cooked. Remove and keep warm.

Add the carrots to the pan and cook for 2 minutes, then add spring onions and snow peas and cook, stirring constantly for 3 minutes. Remove and store with chicken fillets.

Add apple cider to the pan and cook over a high heat, scraping any chicken residue. Boil until reduced to about ½ cup.

Add the cream and mustard and stir through without boiling. Return chicken fillets to pan, warm through and serve immediately with vegetables.

Serves 4

Cheesy Crusted Leg of Lamb

Freshly grated Parmesan cheese gives a far superior flavour to the pre-grated packet variety. If not available try substituting part of the Parmesan with grated non-processed cheddar.

90 g (3 oz) butter
1 cup (2 oz) fresh breadcrumbs
½ cup (2 oz) freshly grated Parmesan cheese
freshly ground black pepper
1.5–2 kg (3–4 lb) leg of lamb
1 small onion, finely diced
1½ cups water
2 stock cubes
1 tablespoon cornflour
3 tablespoons port wine or sweet sherry
salt and pepper to taste

Melt the butter over a medium heat. Add the breadcrumbs, Parmesan and freshly ground black pepper and mix well.

Trim the lamb of all fat. Press the breadcrumb mixture with the palm of the hand over the surface of the lamb. Place in roasting pan and bake 170°C (340°F, Gas Mark 4) for 2–2½ hours (depending on size of leg). Cover with foil if surface should start to scorch. Allow to rest for 20 minutes before carving.

Pour off all but 1 tablespoon of fat from the roasting pan. Add the onion and cook over a moderate heat for 3–4 minutes or until soft and starting to colour. Add water and stock cubes to the pan and stir, scraping in bits that cling to the bottom. Mix cornflour and wine or sherry together, stir into sauce. Bring to the boil and boil for 2–3 minutes.

Strain into a clean saucepan and bring to the boil. Season to taste with salt and pepper.

Carve the leg into thick slices and serve the sauce separately.

Serves 8

Globe Artichokes with Mango Ginger Mayonnaise

An often misunderstood vegetable, it tastes delicious and is best eaten by pulling off the leaves, dipping them into the sauce, then sucking and nibbling the fleshy leaf bases. Discard the leaf tops. Finally, remove the 'choke' of small thistles, and eat the base with any remaining dressing.

4 globe artichokes
lemon slices

Break off any tough outer artichoke leaves and trim the stem quite close to the base leaves. Cut away (with scissors to make it easy) the top third of the artichoke. Place prepared artichoke immediately into water with lemon slices to prevent discolouration.
Cook in boiling salted water for about 15–20 minutes or until the outside leaf pulls easily away from the artichoke. Drain and allow to cool.
Serve with Mango Ginger Mayonnaise, garnished with mango slices.
Serves 4

Mango Ginger Mayonnaise

1 large mango (or 425 g can mango slices)
½ teaspoon freshly grated root ginger
1 cup mayonnaise (preferably made with egg yolks)
2 tablespoons cream

Peel and slice the mango. Reserve 4 slices for garnish.
Place mango, root ginger and mayonnaise in a blender, puree until smooth. Add cream and blend 15 seconds.

Fresh Fruit with Coconut Dipping Cream

A delightful dessert when time or the waistline is precious.

60 g (2 oz) grated or finely chopped coconut cream (block variety)
60 g (2 oz) cream cheese
¼ cup sour cream
3 teaspoons brown sugar
grated rind and juice ½ lemon

Place all ingredients together in a food processor and blend until smooth. Arrange a selection of prepared fresh fruits on individual plates and serve the coconut cream separately in a small bowl as a dipping sauce.

The more exotic the fruit, the more exciting the final result; however it is wiser to choose fruit at its peak of ripeness than to have an unusual fruit for the sake of it — better to have a perfect apple than a bruised or unripe mango.

Suggestions include: strawberries and all berry fruits, kiwi-fruit (Chinese gooseberry), honeydew melon, rock melon (cantaloup) or papaw, grapes, litchis, mangosteen, rhambutan, longans, loquats, mangoes, apples, pears.

Serves 4

Strawberries in Melting Snow Kisses

This recipe may also be assembled in one large croquembouche style arrangement to form a spectacular centre-piece — double all the quantities to form a 25 cm (10 inch) high dessert.

3 egg whites
½ teaspoon cream of tartar
¼ teaspoon salt
¾ cup (6 oz) castor sugar
300 ml (½ pint) cream
1½ tablespoons castor sugar
½ teaspoon vanilla essence
1 punnet strawberries

Beat the egg whites, cream of tartar and salt together until stiff but still glossy. Beat in the sugar, adding a tablespoon at a time. Continue beating until thick.

Spoon or pipe teaspoonfuls of the mixture on to non-stick cooking parchment or lightly greased foil on a scone tray. Allow at least 12 meringues per person.

Bake in a slow oven 140°C (275°F, Gas Mark 1) for 1–1½ hours or until crisp and barely coloured. Cool on a wire rack.

Beat the cream, sugar and vanilla together until stiff. Pile the meringues on to a small plate and assemble them into a mound, using the cream to adhere them. Nestle the strawberries into the cavities.

Serve within 2 hours of assembly as the meringues soften.
Serves 4
Makes approximately 50 meringues

ANNE HADDY (Australia)
Actor (star of *Neighbours*)

Cumquat Rice

This is one of my favourite recipes, but as I am on a low-fat diet I modify it a bit. No added salt — not even when cooking the rice, which I prefer brown. Instead of butter I use chicken stock, or sometimes just heat in a colander over boiling water.

60 g (2 oz) butter
1½ cups (8 oz) brown or white rice
6 cumquats, cut in thin slices and seeds removed
¼ cup (1½ oz) sultanas
1 tablespoon chopped fresh mixed herbs (or 1 teaspoon dried)
salt and freshly ground pepper

Cook the rice in boiling salted water, drain and cool. Melt the butter in a deep frying-pan, add all other ingredients and stir gently until rice is heated through.
Serves 4–6

Note: If cumquats aren't available, use the flesh of half an orange and its finely shredded rind.

ROLF HARRIS (Australia)
Artist and entertainer

Bachelor Scrambled Eggs and Tomatoes

2 eggs and 1 tomato per person
maybe a spring onion if you like them
bits of milk, butter, salt, pepper

First melt small splodge of butter (or margarine) in frying-pan and drop in finely cut up spring onion. Cook over slow heat for short while, then add a slosh of milk — too much and eggs are watery later. Take pan off the heat while you break eggs into pan.

Add a dusting of salt to each egg and as much pepper as you enjoy.

Then, back on to low heat while you graunch up the eggs with a wooden spoon and generally scramble them around. Must be low heat — nothing is worse than little black horribly tasting burnt bits in scrambled egg.

Meanwhile, your tomato should be cut in half and placed under overhead grill — put flat side down first and grill until skin shrivels up and starts to go black, then turn over, add dusting of salt and grill the flat side.

Your scrambled egg should be just starting to solidify, so take it off the heat for a tick while you put in your two beautifully grilled tomatoes. The skin on the smooth side just comes away, but you will need to cut out the core on the other half of the tomato.

Back on the heat while you squelch up the tomato with the wooden spoon. Mix egg and tomato thoroughly. Don't dry it up too much.

DELICIOUS!

BOB HAWKE (Australia)
Prime Minister of Australia

French Onion Soup

To make the real French soup, you should have a good beef stock. Failing that, use beef cubes and water.

6 medium onions
oil or shortening
1 litre (1¾ pints) beef stock

stale bread
grated cheese

Slice the onions thinly — do not chop or mince. Saute in oil or shortening, in small quantities, until brown. Add to heated stock. Repeat the process of browning onions until they are all done. Turn the stock containing the onions down to a simmer, check seasoning and cook for at least 1 hour. In the mean time, make croutons with stale bread and grated cheese in oven or under grill.

Serve in tureen or individual bowls with croutons. The soup can also be gratineed. This means that you sprinkle grated cheese on top of the soup and brown under the grill.

Serves 6

KEN HOM (Hong Kong)
Chinese cookery writer and TV presenter

Rainbow Vegetables in Lettuce Cups

This is my version of a popular Hong Kong dish, one that usually includes minced pigeons or pork. I use only vegetables and draw upon the contrasting textures and flavours to charm the palate while delighting the eye — as the name suggests, this is a multicoloured melange. One does not miss the meat or poultry when one contemplates this rainbow combination and savours the tasty crunchiness of the vegetables combined with crispy fried bean thread noodles, all cupped in a refreshing leaf of lettuce flavoured with hoisin sauce. Be imaginative and substitute other vegetables. Remember to keep the colours sparkling and avoid using too many different ones at the same time — limit yourself to 5 or 6. The garlic is coarsely chopped in this recipe and functions as another vegetable.

500 g (1 lb) lettuce
300 ml (½ pint) oil, preferably ground-nut
30 g (1 oz) bean thread (transparent) noodles
3 tablespoons garlic, coarsely chopped
½ teaspoon salt
2 tablespoons rice wine or dry sherry
3 tablespoons chicken or vegetable stock
125 g (4 oz) carrots, finely diced
250 g (8 oz) zucchini (courgettes), finely diced
125 g (4 oz) red peppers, finely diced
125 g (4 oz) yellow peppers, finely diced
125 g (4 oz) fresh or tinned water chestnuts, coarsely chopped
2 teaspoons light soy sauce
1½ tablespoons oyster sauce
3 tablespoons hoisin sauce

Separate and wash the lettuce leaves, wiping off any excess water, and set them aside.

In a deep-fryer or large wok, heat oil until it is almost smoking. Turn off the heat and deep-fry the noodles until they are crisp and puffed up. Drain them on kitchen paper. (Leave the oil to cool; it can be saved for future use.)

Put 1 tablespoon of the oil in which you have fried the noodles into a wok or frying-pan and heat it. Add the garlic, salt, rice wine, stock and carrots and stir-fry for about 2 minutes. Then add the rest of the vegetables (except the lettuce) and water chestnuts together with the soy sauce and continue to stir-fry for 3 minutes. Stir in the oyster sauce and continue to stir-fry for 1 minute more.

Turn the mixture on to a platter. Arrange the lettuce and noodles each on separate platters, put the hoisin sauce in a small bowl, and serve at once.

Serves 4–6

Crispy Vegetarian Wuntuns

Wuntuns stuffed with tasty fillings of meat or flavourful vegetables are universally appreciated. One of the more popular versions is the deep-fried crispy crackling morsel with the juicy spicy stuffing within. This is a vegetarian version of a traditional Chinese treat, the stuffing composed of carrots, cabbage and bean sprouts, with some bean curd for body. These wuntuns are delicious with hoisin sauce or, if you prefer, a dipping sauce made with your own combinations of chilli oil, white rice wine vinegar and light soy sauce. They are ideal with drinks or as a starter.

Do not make them too far ahead of time. Because they are made with a moisture-laden vegetable stuffing, the wuntun skins will soften in an unpalatable way if they are allowed to sit for too long a time. Make them and serve them straight away.

1 packet wuntun skins (about 30–35)
450 ml (15 fl. oz) oil, preferably ground-nut
hoisin sauce for dipping

Filling
1 tablespoon oil, preferably ground-nut
2 tablespoons garlic, finely chopped
125 g (4 oz) cabbage, finely shredded
60 g (2 oz) carrots, finely shredded
60 g (2 oz) bean sprouts
1 tablespoon dark soy sauce
3 tablespoons bean curd, mashed
1 teaspoon sugar
½ teaspoon salt
1 teaspoon sesame oil
½ teaspoon freshly ground black pepper

Heat the oil in a wok or large frying-pan until it is moderately hot. Add the garlic, cabbage, carrots and bean sprouts and stir-fry for 1 minute. Set it aside to cool thoroughly.

Combine the cooled vegetables with the rest of the filling ingredients and mix well. Then, using a teaspoon, put a small amount of filling in the centre of each wuntun skin. Bring up two sides, dampen the edges with a little water and pinch them together to make a triangle. Fold over the bottom two corners and press together. The filling should be well sealed in.

Heat the oil in a deep-fryer or large wok until it is hot. Deep-fry the filled wuntun in several batches and drain each batch on kitchen paper. Serve at once with hoisin sauce.
Makes 30–35

FRANK IFIELD (Britain)
Singer

Lamingtons 'Bessie's Beauties'

My grandfather was a baker, so my grandmother learnt to cook delicious cakes. This is one of Gran's specialities.

Make a basic butter cake recipe and bake in a greased slab tin 25 cm (10 inches) square in a moderate oven 180°C (350°F, Gas Mark 4) for 35–40 minutes, or buy a ready-made plain cake.

When the cake is cold cut into squares and dip each square into slightly warm chocolate icing, then roll in desiccated coconut and leave to dry on a cake cooler.

Icing
2 teaspoons butter
¼ cup boiling water
500 g (1 lb) icing sugar
60 g (2 oz) cocoa
vanilla essence
250 g (½ lb) desiccated coconut

Dissolve butter in boiling water and cool slightly. Sift icing sugar and cocoa together and blend into liquid, mixing to required consistency. If not thin enough add a little more water. Flavour with vanilla. The icing should be fairly thin.

The squares of cake can be dipped into the icing on a fork to coat on all sides, or the icing can be spooned over the squares until coated. Roll each square in coconut while the icing is still damp, then leave to dry completely on a rack.

ALAN JONES (Australia)
Motor racing driver

Bolognese Sauce a la Alan

oil	1 tablespoon oregano
2 large onions, chopped	1 tablespoon basil
3 cloves garlic	500 g (1 lb) mince
8 peppercorns	1–2 cans tomatoes
8 whole cloves	1 small can tomato puree

Heat oil and fry onions and garlic. Add peppercorns, cloves, oregano and basil. Add mince and fry until cooked through. Add tomatoes and puree.

You can also add sliced zucchini, capsicum, mushrooms, celery.

Pizza

185 g (6 oz) self-raising flour	garlic
60 g (2 oz) soft margarine	oregano
milk	canned tomatoes
oil	canned tomato puree
4 rashers bacon, chopped	grated cheese
1 onion, chopped	

Rub together flour and margarine, add milk. Make into dough. Roll and put on greased ovenproof plate.

Fry oil, bacon, onion, garlic, oregano, tomatoes and puree. Pour mixture on top of dough, then add good quantity of grated cheese. Cook at 190°C (375°F, Gas Mark 5) for 20–25 minutes.

BERNARD KING (Australia)
Cookery writer, TV personality

Silverside — An Old Favourite

Tune in all you young trendies, all you upwardly mobile types, it's all proving to be just as Mother said — if you keep a thing long enough you'll need it again. Silverside or corned beef is coming back! Actually it's never been forgotten at my table, but then that's my bush-whacker style.

The big chunk of corned beef can be a handsome performer, a welcome change, and as easy as a trip to the deli! You must have a large pot, so suggest to those mean-as-the-proverbial aunts that they skip the casseroles and club in for one cauldron. Even if they're desperately cheap the common aluminium will do.

Order the beef well ahead to be sure the butcher has time for deep soaking — thorough penetration of the brine is essential. For hot serving allow three hours of cooking at least. Settle the beef in the cauldron and cover with cold water. Add a couple of onions, some bay-leaves and some cloves. Now simmer (and stress simmer only) with the lid on until the meat is fork tender. The piece is ready to present.

Those with more aspirations to the giddy heights of glamour could finish with a glaze — any you'd use for ham are successful. For informal offering, the companions need be only some hot crusty damper (or some of my savoury pumpkin scones) and a salad assortment. For more individual reaction from the beef, try these changes to the simmering stock.
- Mix together equal quantities of water and grapefruit juice — you achieve a marvellous tang to the meat — keep the key a deep dark family secret.
- Sometimes I'll add a dark cumquat or orange marmalade to the simmering stock — another subtle success.
- Try this for a different finish. Cook the meat a day ahead. When the meat is ready set out several sheets of foil, drain the meat and place the piece on the foil. Now spread chilli powder very liberally all over the outside. Rub the chilli well in then wrap and seal as tightly as you can. Then wrap again in a tea towel tied tightly. Refrigerate the piece ready for a reheat or cold serve the next day.

You'll be delighted to find that you've achieved an almost pastrami-like taste — delicious with pickles and people!

The State-of-the-Art Barbecue

Some of the top 400 are still raising eyebrows at my staging several barbecue parties recently. For some reason they presume that the ordinariness of the barbecue is less than BK Style — however, they have not given me credit for elevating the domestic to the divine, for making a work of art from a pig's ear, so to speak.

My barbecue is scarcely Fred style — I don't allow anyone to stack all the food on the griddle all at the same time. I certainly begin the procedure, the initial preparation, several days before, and I most definitely offer elegant taste experiences for all. The essence of the art lies in the marinade — and the fastidious dressing of the product.

All meat — beef, pork or venison — must be allowed several days to saturate in whatever marinade I've designed for the event. All those cuts are thoroughly trimmed of fats and sinews before being sliced into fine slivers to encourage deep penetration of flavour and to accelerate the cooking. Seafood products accept flavour more readily than the meats so shorter marinade times are necessary.

On the day I operate at least two griddles — one for the meats, one for the seafoods. I encourage guests to select a morsel with chopsticks, drop it on the griddle, turn once in a moment, then wrap the item in foliage or devour with a chunky bread-roll.

The whole system moves your guests about, increasing the social character of the event, encouraging party chatter, helping the flow. People don't over-eat, the food is not over-cooked, it all works wonderfully. Furthermore I find guests return later to snack again.

The easing of pressure on both the host and his kitchen crew is so appreciated — and everyone loves the fare.

Thus be reassured that, when you see reports of a BK barbecue, the occasion will most certainly be well above average, far above the ordinary — perhaps even marked for greatness!

RUSTIE LEE (Britain)
Caribbean cook

Ackee and Salt Fish

At last, something that the Queen and I have in common —our favourite Caribbean dish, which is almost the national dish of Jamaica. Ackee grows on a tree and is the flesh found in the seed pods.

500 g (1 lb) salt fish (cod will do well)
1 can ackee
125 g (4 oz) margarine or butter
2 rashers bacon
2 tomatoes
1 onion
1 sweet pepper
½ teaspoon thyme
pepper and salt to taste
parsley to garnish

Boil salt fish for 15 minutes, or soak in cold water overnight. Wash to remove salt. Open tin of ackee and drain.
Melt margarine or butter in pan and fry bacon for 3 minutes. Chop remaining ingredients and saute in pan for 5 minutes. Shred fish and add to the pan for another 5 minutes. Lastly add ackee and cook for a further 5 minutes.
Garnish with parsley.

Ham and Egg Pasta Savoury

A delicious supper dish.

250 g (½ lb) shell pasta
1.2 litres (2 pints) milk
60 g (2 oz) flour
60 g (2 oz) butter
1 kg (2 lb) ham
2 tablespoons chopped parsley
375 g (¾ lb) mild cheddar cheese, grated
2 teaspoons salt
1 teaspoon black pepper
4–6 eggs, hard-boiled

Cook the pasta shells for 10–12 minutes in salted boiling water. Drain the water away.
Place ½ cup of the milk in a saucepan. Mix the flour and butter together, blend gently into the milk in little balls, and continue adding the milk.

Then whisk together to form a smooth white sauce. Add salt and pepper to taste.

Chop all the ham into squares. Halve the sauce. Add parsley, half the grated cheese, all the ham and pasta to one half of the sauce.

Slice the eggs and smooth a knob of butter on the pie dish. Then arrange the egg slices around the dish and pour mixture into the middle of the arrangement. Pour the remaining white sauce over the top. Sprinkle the rest of the cheese over and bake in a moderate oven for 15–20 minutes. Garnish with parsley and serve with a salad.

Pineapple and Mango Pie

Ideal for those long, hot summer days — if they ever come!

Pastry
500 g (1 lb) plain flour
250 g (½ lb) butter
½ cup (4 oz) castor sugar
2 eggs

Filling
1 fresh pineapple
1 large mango
300 ml (½ pint) water
½ cup (4 oz) castor sugar
1 teaspoon cinnamon
1 teaspoon vanilla essence
3 teaspoons cornflour
⅓ cup (2 oz) icing sugar (for dusting)

First make the pastry. Sieve the flour and rub in the butter. Add the sugar and rub that in. Mould together with eggs. Divide in two. Roll out one piece and line a 30 cm (12 inch) flan dish. Bake blind (with greaseproof paper in the centre containing beans or bread crusts) at 190°C (375°F, Gas Mark 5) for 10 minutes.

Cut top off pineapple and keep for decoration. Peel and chop flesh of both pineapple and mango. Cook for 5 minutes with water, sugar, cinnamon and essence. Blend cornflour in a little of the liquid, then stir into mixture to thicken.

Remove pastry from oven and put mango and pineapple filling inside. Roll the rest of the pastry to make pie lid. Cover the pie, cut slits in the top, and bake for 20–25 minutes. Remove from oven and allow to cool.

Decorate with pineapple top and dust with icing sugar. Serve with fresh cream or ice-cream.

Rustie's Aphrodisiac

Who can resist my famous aphrodisiac? It's almost always guaranteed to work, even on hopeless cases . . .

1 papaw
1 mango
1 ripe banana
½ cup (4 oz) sugar
½ small tin condensed milk
300 ml (½ pint) water
3 ice cubes
3 tots dark rum
½ teaspoon ground nutmeg

    Peel papaw and remove seeds. Cut fruit into large segments. Peel mango, cut flesh from seed and dice into small segments. Peel and dice banana.
    Place fruit in a liquidiser with sugar and milk. Beat until smooth. Add water, ice cubes, and finally rum. Beat again until very smooth, then serve in chilled glasses.

JUDY McCALLUM (Australia)
Artist

Macadamia Pumpkin

½ cup (2 oz) macadamia nuts, chopped coarsely
3 small butternut pumpkins
salt and pepper
2 tablespoons butter
½ cup finely chopped onions
½ cup (1 oz) breadcrumbs
½ cup (2 oz) grated cheese
¼ cup (1½ oz) sultanas
½ teaspoon ground cardamom
1 egg
1 cup cream

    Pre-heat oven to moderate. Place macadamias in oven until golden brown (careful — they burn easily).
    Cut tops off pumpkins and keep them for 'lids'. Scoop out the seeds and filaments. Season the pumpkin with salt and pepper.

Melt butter, add onion, cook until soft.

Mix all ingredients except cream. Fill pumpkins with mixture, then add ⅓ cup cream to each. Replace tops. Bake for 1 hour or until pumpkin is tender on outside and bubbling on inside.

Cut into thick wedges. Serve with hot greens or tossed salad.

LEO McKERN (Australia)
Actor

Leo's Breakfast

This is probably one of the quickest, if not *the* quickest, prepared and cooked meal in the history of culinary art. It must be followed *exactly*. (Note remark about butter, principally.)

Take a small saucepan, a knob of butter (*not* margarine) of about a dessertspoon size, and put on a *hot* heat source until butter is burning *black* — don't become faint-hearted and settle for light brown — and at this stage tip in two seasoned eggs previously broken into a cup. At once whip with a fork while removing from heat source. The boiling butter should cook the eggs immediately. Cynics will say 'Huh! — scrambled egg!' I can assure them the flavour comparison with your usual English breakfast dish is chalk and cheese.

KEITH MICHELL (Australia), From *Practically Macrobiotic*
Actor

Pancakes with Bechamel Vegetable Sauce

Sauce
1 cup chopped white cabbage
1 small carrot, finely diced
½ cup chopped scallions
 (spring onions)
½ cup bean sprouts

1 tablespoon kuzu
1 cup soy milk
pinch salt
1 tablespoon rice vinegar
1 cup water

Boil cabbage, carrot, scallions and bean sprouts gently in water for 5 minutes.

Mix kuzu in soy milk with salt and rice vinegar and add to the vegetables to thicken. Bring to a boil, stirring until sauce thickens. Turn off heat.

Pancakes
1 cup wholewheat pastry flour
pinch salt
1 cup cold soy milk

1 cup cold water
1 free-range egg
1 tablespoon sesame oil

½ cup chopped parsley for garnish

Mix the ingredients quickly to a thin creamy consistency and let stand in a cool place for at least 1 hour.

Brush a little corn oil on skillet. Heat gently but it should not be too hot. To test the heat of your skillet, let a few drops of water fall on it. If the water stays and boils the surface is not hot enough; if it vanishes quickly it is too hot. The water should bounce and spitter.

Drop in the pancake mixture. Pancakes should not be too thick.

Place one pancake on a plate and cover with sauce. Add next pancake on top of this, cover with sauce, and repeat until last pancake is used. Garnish with any remaining sauce, decorate with parsley and serve. Slice as you would a cake.

NATIONAL TRUST OF AUSTRALIA (VICTORIA) (Australia),
From *Tried & Trusted*

Manor House Beef

1 fillet of beef
¾–1 cup water

Marinade
1 clove garlic
1 tablespoon honey
⅓ cup dry sherry
2 tablespoons soy sauce
piece of green ginger grated

1 tablespoon cornflour
2 teaspoons chicken stock powder

2 teaspoons curry powder
1 teaspoon bicarbonate of soda
2 teaspoons sugar
2 teaspoons ground black pepper

Blend marinade in a bowl. Pour over fillet and cover, marinating for at least 2 hours.

Drain as much marinade as possible from fillet. Brown fillet on all sides. Roast as desired in a hot oven — possibly 20–30 minutes.

Place remaining marinade in small saucepan. Blend cornflour in water and add to marinade with stock powder. Stir until sauce thickens. Place in jug and serve with fillet.

JOHN NEWCOMBE (Australia)
Tennis professional

Impossible Quiche

4 eggs
90 g (3 oz) soft butter
½ cup (2 oz) plain flour
2 cups milk

250 g (8 oz) tin salmon or tuna
1 onion, finely chopped
salt and pepper
grated cheese

Blend eggs, butter, flour and milk in mixer and pour into buttered 25 cm (10 inch) pie plate.

Add salmon (deboned) or tuna, onion, salt and pepper; sprinkle with grated cheese.

Bake in moderate oven 180°C (350°F, Gas Mark 4) for 35–40 minutes until set.

Different fillings may be used — e.g. bacon, onion and cheese, asparagus and cheese, mushrooms and cheese, etc.

Miracle Pie

1 cup (7 oz) sugar
1 cup (3 oz) desiccated coconut
½ cup (2 oz) plain flour
4 eggs

125 g (4 oz) soft butter
2 teaspoons vanilla
2 cups milk

Beat all ingredients together in a bowl until well blended. Pour into greased pie dish. Bake for one hour at 180°C (350°F, Gas Mark 4).

It comes out with crusty top, custard in the middle and soft pastry underneath.

BERT NEWTON (Australia)
Radio and TV personality

Savoury Steak and Noodles

This is just to prove that Aussies know a little more about steak than simply grilling it with a couple of fried eggs!

1 kg (2 lb) topside beef
1 teaspoon flour
1 teaspoon sugar
¼ teaspoon nutmeg
¼ teaspoon pepper
1 packet French onion soup

3 cups water
1 teaspoon vinegar
1 teaspoon Worcestershire sauce
a little Gravox
about 1 tablespoon cornflour

Chop topside in cubes, roll in flour, sugar, nutmeg and pepper. Put in saucepan. Cover with onion soup. Add water, vinegar and Worcestershire sauce. Simmer 1½–2 hours. Thicken with Gravox and cornflour blended in a little water when cooked.

PATTI NEWTON (Australia)
Radio and TV personality

Tuna Casserole

This recipe particularly appeals to me because it takes advantage of the much-underrated tuna fish and requires ingredients that are usually in the kitchen waiting for us!

470 g (15 oz) can tuna, drained and flaked
315 g (10 oz) can cream of celery soup
1 onion, peeled and grated
2 sticks celery, chopped
½ teaspoon grated lemon rind
2 tablespoons lemon juice
2 tablespoons chopped parsley
salt and pepper
315 g (10 oz) can whole kernel corn, drained
packaged dry breadcrumbs
1 cup (2 oz) fresh breadcrumbs
30 g (1 oz) butter

Put tuna, undiluted soup, onion, celery, lemon rind and juice, parsley, salt, pepper and corn in bowl. Mix well.

Grease an ovenproof dish, dust lightly with dry breadcrumbs. Spoon tuna mixture into dish. Toss fresh breadcrumbs in melted butter, sprinkle over the top.

Bake in moderate oven 25–30 minutes.

Serves 4

GREG NORMAN (Australia)
Golfing professional

Oriental Beef

750 g (1½ lb) rump steak
1 egg
¼ cup (1 oz) cornflour
1 teaspoon salt
pepper
3 sticks celery
2 large carrots

1 red pepper
1 green pepper
2 medium onions
½ cup oil
1 tablespoon arrowroot
2 cups stock
1 tablespoon soy sauce

Cut steak into thin strips. Beat egg, cornflour, salt and pepper until a smooth paste. Add meat and cover each piece with batter.

Cut celery into 2.5 cm (1 inch) pieces and carrots into thin strips. Cut pepper into cubes and onions into rings.

Heat oil in frying-pan and fry meat until golden brown and drain. Pour off excess oil and cook vegetables for 2 minutes. Add stock and steak to vegetables and bring to boil. Blend arrowroot and soy sauce, stir in and cook until sauce thickens. Add meat and reheat.

Serves 6–8

KERRY PACKER (Australia)
Chairman, Consolidated Press Holdings Limited

Oysters with Three Toppings

From *The Australian Women's Weekly Light and Luscious Summertime Cookbook*, published November 1986

Australia is famous for its fine seafood — oysters are readily available and deliciously plump. Simply serve them in their shells on a bed of ice accompanied by buttered bread, lemon wedges and freshly ground black pepper. For those who like their oysters dressed up, here are different ways of serving them. Each topping will be enough for 12 oysters — adapt the quantities to suit yourself.

Basil Butter

60 g (2 oz) butter
2 tablespoons chopped fresh basil
2 tablespoons grated Parmesan cheese
1 clove garlic, crushed
¼ cup (1 oz) grated Parmesan cheese, extra

Have butter at room temperature, beat in bowl until smooth. Stir in basil, cheese and garlic. Divide over 12 oysters, top with extra cheese, grill until butter is melted.

Bacon and Tomato Topping

2 bacon rashers, chopped finely
2 tablespoons tomato paste
1 tablespoon vodka
1 teaspoon Worcestershire sauce

Combine all ingredients in bowl, divide over 12 oysters, grill until bacon is crisp and golden brown.

Sour Cream Topping

30 g (1 oz) butter
1 tablespoon oil
1 clove garlic, crushed
1 cup (2 oz) stale breadcrumbs
½ cup sour cream
¼ cup (1 oz) grated Mozzarella cheese
2 teaspoons lemon juice

    Heat butter, oil and garlic in pan, add crumbs, stir constantly over heat until golden brown. Combine sour cream, cheese and lemon juice in bowl, divide over 12 oysters. Sprinkle with crumbs, grill oysters until topping is crisp.

Crusty Cheese Damper

From *The Australian Women's Weekly Easy Entertaining Cookbook*, published November 1985

Damper is a party bread substitute. It is best served hot, straight from the oven.

4 cups (1 lb) self-raising flour
2½ cups milk, approximately
1 cup (4 oz) grated tasty cheese
1 teaspoon dry mustard
1 tablespoon sesame seeds

    Sift flour into bowl, stir in enough milk to give a sticky dough. Knead on lightly floured surface until smooth, shape into a round. Place dough on to lightly greased oven tray, press out with fingers to about 3 cm (1¼ inch) thick. Using a sharp knife mark into 10 wedges, cut wedges into dough about 1 cm (½ inch) deep.
    Sprinkle dough with combined cheese and mustard, top with sesame seeds. Bake in hot oven 15 minutes; reduce heat to moderately hot and bake a further 20 minutes or until golden brown and damper sounds hollow when tapped with fingers.

Tropical Trifle

From *The Australian Women's Weekly Easy Entertaining Cookbook*, published November 1985

Use the fruit — fresh or canned — of your choice to decorate the trifle. We used mango, kiwi-fruit and passionfruit. The cake, jelly and custard layers of the trifle can be completed, covered and refrigerated up to two days ahead of serving time if desired. Decorate with fruit and whipped cream up to several hours before serving time.

1 Swiss roll
½ cup sweet sherry
2 packets lemon jelly crystals
1½ cups boiling water
1½ cups cold water
custard
fruit and whipped cream to decorate

Cut Swiss roll into slices, place over base of serving dish. Sprinkle with sherry. Add boiling water to jelly crystals, stir until dissolved, stir in cold water. Pour over Swiss roll, refrigerate until almost set. Pour custard over jelly, refrigerate. Decorate with fruit and whipped cream.

Swiss Roll

3 eggs, separated
½ cup (4 oz) castor sugar
¾ cup (3 oz) self-raising flour
2 tablespoons hot milk
extra castor sugar
¾ cup lemon butter

Beat egg whites in small bowl with electric mixer until soft peaks form; gradually beat in sugar until dissolved. Beat in egg yolks. Transfer mixture to large bowl, lightly fold in sifted flour and hot milk. Pour mixture into greased and lined Swiss roll pan, base measuring 25 x 30 cm (10 x 12 inches).

Bake in hot oven 8 minutes or until browned. While sponge is cooking, place a sheet of greaseproof paper on table, sprinkle lightly with extra castor sugar. When sponge is cooked, turn quickly on to paper, peel off lining paper. Cut off crisp edges from long sides. Spread sponge evenly with lemon butter, roll up loosely with the help of the greaseproof paper. Lift roll on to wire rack to cool.

Custard

1 cup (4 oz) custard powder
1 cup (7 oz) sugar
3 cups milk
300 ml (½ pint) thickened (double) cream
2 teaspoons vanilla essence
4 egg yolks

Combine custard powder and sugar in pan, gradually stir in milk. Stir constantly over heat until mixture boils and thickens. Remove from heat, stir in cream, vanilla essence and egg yolks. Cover, cool to room temperature.

SARA PASTON-WILLIAMS (Britain)
Cookery writer

Likky Soup

This is a favourite Cornish soup made from leeks, which are a very popular vegetable in the West Country.

60 g (2 oz) butter
3–4 medium leeks, chopped
1 medium onion, chopped
4 medium potatoes, peeled and chopped
1.5 litres (2½ pints) chicken stock
salt and freshly milled black pepper
pinch grated nutmeg
150 ml (¼ pint) (single) cream
fresh parsley or chives, chopped

Heat the butter in a large saucepan until it is foaming. Add the leeks and onion, stir them well until they are buttery and then cover the pan with a lid. Leave to 'sweat' on a gentle heat for about 10 minutes or until the vegetables are soft but not coloured. Add the potatoes and mix well.

Gradually add the stock, seasoning and nutmeg. Cover again and simmer for about 20–25 minutes, or until the potato is tender. Liquidise the soup at this point if you wish. Taste and adjust the seasoning as necessary.

Finally, add the cream and serve garnished with parsley or chives.
Serves 6

Aunty Glad's Cornish Pasty

It is said that the devil has never crossed the River Tamar into Cornwall for fear that he might be made into a pasty! Indeed, Cornish women have in the past put almost anything into a pasty, both sweet and savoury, and even today the Cornish pasty is the staple dish of the county. Pasties are made according to individual taste and are often marked in one corner with the owner's initials; then, if it is not eaten up at lunch-time, it can be consumed later by its rightful owner. The true Cornish way to eat a pasty is to hold it in your hand and start eating at one end.

125 g (4 oz) shortcrust pastry
90 g (3 oz) lean chuck steak
½ small onion
60 g (2 oz) potato
30–60 g (1–2 oz) turnip
salt and freshly milled black pepper
15 g (½ oz) butter
beaten egg and milk to glaze

Roll the pastry into a round approximately 6 mm (¼ inch) thick, using a 17.5 cm (7 inch) plate as a guide if you wish. Cut the meat into little pieces and chop the onion finely. Slice the potato into penny-sized flakes and chop the turnip into small pieces.

Place a layer of potato, followed by a layer of meat, then onion and turnip, on to the pastry round. (Don't mix the pastry filling beforehand.) Season well with salt and pepper and add the knob of butter. Fold the pastry over and crimp the edges to form a good seal. Make a small hole in the top of the pasty to let the steam escape during cooking. Glaze with beaten egg and milk and place on a greased baking sheet.

Bake near the top of a fairly hot oven at 200°C (400°F, Gas Mark 6) for 10 minutes, then reduce the oven temperature to 180°C (350°F, Gas Mark 4). Continue cooking for a further 35 minutes, or until golden brown. The pasty is delicious hot or cold, and will stay warm for some time after cooking if you wrap it in a clean cloth, tea-towel or kitchen foil.
Makes 1

Squab Pie

The origins of this ancient pie date back to medieval days when sweet and savoury tastes were combined. It is often associated with the West Country where, since the eighteenth century, it has been traditional to spoon clotted cream into, or over, the pie just before serving. A 'squab' is a young unfledged pigeon, and in the past this is what went into the pie. Sometimes, on the coastal areas, young skinned cormorants were used instead. In more recent recipes the pigeons are replaced by mutton or lamb, or are mixed with the meat. Sliced apples and onions are included and, in some recipes, currants or prunes are also added. The pie is spiced with nutmeg, mace or cinnamon and often includes sugar or honey and cider. A lid of puff, rough or shortcrust pastry completes the pie, and it is eaten hot with clotted cream.

1 kg (2 lb) lean stewing lamb
500 g (1 lb) onions
500 g (1 lb) cooking apples
1 teaspoon dried mixed herbs
pinch ground mace
pinch ground nutmeg
salt and freshly milled black pepper
250 g (½ lb) puff or rough puff pastry
beaten egg and milk to glaze
125 g (4 oz) clotted cream

Trim the meat of fat and bone and cut into small cubes. Peel and slice the onions; peel, core and slice the apples. Layer the onions, apples and meat in a deep 1.2 litre (2 pint) pie dish. Sprinkle with herbs and spice and season well. Cover the pie dish with pastry in the normal way. Make a slit in the top of the pie and brush with beaten egg and milk.

Bake near the top of a fairly hot oven at 190°C (375°F, Gas Mark 5) for 20 minutes until the pastry is brown, then reduce the temperature to 160°C (325°F, Gas Mark 3) and cook the pie on a lower shelf for a further 55–60 minutes or until the meat is tender. If the pastry seems to be browning too quickly, cover loosely with foil to protect it. (The juices from the meat, onions and apple make a stock which can be drained from the pie, thickened and poured back if you wish, but it is very good unthickened.)

Just before serving, spoon the clotted cream into the pie — either through the slit in the pastry lid or by removing a portion of pastry and replacing it after the cream has been added. Serve hot with boiled potatoes, a green vegetable, and hot beetroot or red cabbage.

Serves 6

Cornish Burnt Cream

Burnt cream is a delicious West Country dish which has been made for centuries. Original recipes for this delicacy suggest layering baked custard with clotted cream, but one layer of cream on the top is sufficiently rich, I think you will find. Very thinly sliced citron was traditionally placed on top of the cream before the sugar, but sliced strawberries underneath the custard are excellent. Start making the pudding the day before you want to serve it.

125–185 g (4–6 oz) fresh strawberries, hulled
600 ml (1 pint) thickened (double) cream
1 vanilla pod, split
6 egg yolks
30 g (1 oz) castor sugar
125 g (4 oz) clotted cream
castor sugar for topping

Slice the prepared strawberries and place on absorbent kitchen paper to remove excess juice. Then spread the fruit evenly over the bottom of a shallow fireproof dish, or dishes if you are making individual creams.

Put the cream and vanilla pod in the top of a double saucepan if you have one, or in an ordinary saucepan. Cover and bring to scalding point, but do not let it boil. Meanwhile, work the egg yolks with the sugar in a basin until they are light in colour. Remove the vanilla pod and pour the cream on to the egg yolk mixture, whisking continuously until well mixed. Return to the top of the double saucepan or arrange the basin over a pan of boiling water, over a gentle heat. Slowly and gently stir the cream continuously until it is quite thick and the whisk leaves a definite trail. On no account let it boil. Strain into the prepared dish or dishes. Allow the cream to cool completely before putting into the refrigerator for 6–8 hours, or preferably overnight to set right through.

One or two hours before serving, spread the top of the pudding with a layer of clotted cream. Pre-heat the grill until it is red-hot. Using a sugar dredger, coat the top of the cream with an even layer of castor sugar about 6 mm (¼ inch) thick (2–3 tablespoons). Wipe the edges of the dish clean and stand it on a metal tray or rack. Put under the pre-heated grill and carefully watch it until the sugar has melted completely and taken on a golden colour. Remove from the heat and leave in a cool place until needed, but don't put in the refrigerator as this will soften the crisp top.

Just before serving crack the hard caramel layer and decorate the top with crystallised red or pink rose petals and leaves, or extra strawberries and a few strawberry leaves and flowers. Place on a doily-covered plate. Another pretty idea is to serve the pudding surrounded by deep red rose petals.

Serves 6

ERIC PEARCE (Australia)
TV personality

Fruity Shepherds Pie

500 g (1 lb) minced steak
2 onions, finely chopped
2 tomatoes, peeled and chopped
1 banana, sliced
½ cup pineapple pieces, drained
60 g (2 oz) raisins, chopped
1 tablespoon tomato sauce
2 tablespoons Worcestershire sauce
salt and pepper
½ teaspoon nutmeg
30 g (1 oz) flour
1 cup water or stock
500 g (1 lb) mashed potatoes
60 g (2 oz) tasty cheese, grated

Fry meat and onions till changed colour. Add tomatoes, banana, pineapple, raisins, sauces, seasonings.
Blend flour in water or stock, add to meat mixture, stir till cooked. Pour into casserole dish, cover with mashed potato, sprinkle with grated cheese.
Bake in moderate oven 30–40 minutes.

JEAN PENMAN (Australia)
Wife of the Archbishop of Melbourne

Apricot Mustard Glazed Corned Silverside

> Australians are fortunate in having available a marvellous variety of meat which encourages creative meat cookery. Silverside is an economical cut of meat which makes this dish an excellent one for entertaining or for family use. It is best served at room temperature.

1½–2 kg (3–4 lb) corned silverside (choose a long narrow piece in preference to a thick short piece)
1–2 onions
whole cloves
whole peppercorns

Glaze
¼ cup apricot jam
1 teaspoon prepared hot English mustard
½ teaspoon freshly ground black pepper

Place meat in a large saucepan with whole peeled onions and a few cloves and peppercorns. Cover with water. Bring to the boil gently and simmer for about 2 hours.
Prepare glaze by mixing together all ingredients. Lift meat out of saucepan and place in baking dish. Spread glaze all over upper surface of meat. Bake 20 minutes in a moderate oven till topping is bubbly.

Spicy Beef Curry

> The Archbishop and I have lived and worked in Pakistan, where our taste for curry was kindled. Today's Australia is a diverse multicultural community which allows scope for every kind of cooking. The addition of side dishes, salads, chutneys and yoghurt, along with flat bread (chuppaty) and poppadam as an alternative to rice, will enhance your meal.

1 tablespoon oil
¼ cup (1 oz) slivered almonds
2 onions, chopped
2 cloves garlic, crushed
2.5 cm (1 inch) green (fresh) ginger, chopped
1 teaspoon ground cumin
1 teaspoon ground coriander
1 teaspoon ground cardamom
1 teaspoon ground black pepper
2 teaspoons poppy seeds
½ teaspoon turmeric
¼ teaspoon chillies (crushed or powdered)

¼ teaspoon salt
1 kg (2 lb) beef or mutton, cubed
¼ cup yoghurt
1 cup water or stock

Heat oil and lightly fry almonds; remove and reserve for garnish.
Add onions, garlic and ginger to hot oil and fry until lightly golden. Combine all spices and stir in. Add meat and brown. Add yoghurt and water or stock.
Cover and cook slowly till meat is tender (about 1½–2 hours), stirring occasionally. Add a little more liquid if necessary during cooking.
Garnish with almonds and/or onion rings.

THE RITZ (Britain)
Head Chef David Miller

Dressed Crab
(Entree)

3 x 1250 g (2½ lb) boiled crabs
1½ cups (3 oz) white breadcrumbs
1 head lettuce
salt and pepper
3 hard-boiled eggs
3 tablespoons chopped parsley
paprika
2 whole lemons

Remove claws from body and crack the shell. Very carefully remove white meat, making sure you have no shell with it, and refrigerate.
To remove the body, pull the legs and the middle out. Clean the inside, remove the intestines. Then remove the brown meat, which is tucked under the inside of the shell. Wash out the shells, making sure they are very clean, and refrigerate.

Mix the brown meat with the breadcrumbs and season to taste.
Slice the lettuce into thin strips and place into the shells.
Lightly season the white meat and place at both ends of the shells, leaving approximately 2.5 cm (1 inch) gap in the middle. Fill with the brown meat and arrange decoratively.
Separate the whites from the egg yolks and pass them through a sieve separately. Place the egg and parsley in three individual lines on both sides of the brown meat.
Refrigerate until serving.
Serve with lemon mayonnaise or just fresh lemon.
Serves 6

Lemon Mayonnaise

2 egg yolks
1 teaspoon dry English mustard
¼ teaspoon salt
freshly ground black pepper (few twists of mill)
1 pinch castor sugar
300 ml (½ pint) salad oil
2 tablespoons white wine vinegar
1 or 2 lemons

Beat the eggs until thick; add the mustard, salt, pepper and sugar.
Whisk the eggs vigorously. Add the oil drop by drop until it is absorbed completely.
As the mayonnaise thickens it becomes shiny. Finally, blend in the vinegar.
If serving lemon mayonnaise add fresh lemon juice to taste (about half a lemon per person).
Yields 300 ml (½ pint)

Guinea Fowl Broth, Enhanced with Tarragon and Forest Mushrooms

Basic Stock
2 x 1250 g (2½ lb) fresh guinea fowls
1 kg (2 lb) chicken bones
1 onion
250 g (8 oz) carrots
125 g (4 oz) celery
125 g (4 oz) leeks
bouquet garni
white peppercorns
tarragon stalks or parsley
salt

Remove flesh from guinea fowls and refrigerate.
Roughly chop the vegetables. Roast guinea fowl and chicken bones in the oven with the vegetables until brown. Place in a boiling pan and cover with 4.8 litres (8 pints) of water. Add the bouquet garni, white peppercorns, tarragon stalks and a little salt and bring to the boil. Leave to simmer, slowly removing scum from the surface.
When reduced by half remove from heat and pass through fine sieve or muslin and leave to cool.

Clarification
guinea fowl meat (keep one breast for garnish)
125 g (4 oz) onions
125 g (4 oz) leeks
125 g (4 oz) celery
125 g (4 oz) mushrooms
¼ bunch tarragon (or 1 teaspoon dried leaves)
8 egg whites
2.4 litres (4 pints) stock
60 g (2 oz) tomato puree

Mince the meat, vegetables and herbs together. Add the egg whites and whisk together.

Place in a large pot together with the stock and tomato puree. Whisk again until froth forms on the surface.

When broth starts to boil, reduce heat and simmer slowly for 1½–2 hours. Do not let this broth reach boiling point at any time or it will cloud the broth. Strain through a layer of muslin cloth into a bowl, then strain again through a clean piece of muslin. It should then be perfectly clear.

Serves 6

To Garnish Broth
1 breast of guinea fowl
60 g (2 oz) mushrooms
fresh tarragon leaves

Roast the breast of guinea fowl in foil, then slice it in thin pieces. Thinly slice the mushrooms and chop the tarragon. Place a little of each into the serving dishes and pour boiling broth over when serving.

Note: The stock can be made 48 hours before and kept in the fridge. If you wish you can also clarify it beforehand and refrigerate it overnight.

Prime Roast Rib of Scottish Beef with Yorkshire Pudding

3–4 kg (6–8 lb) prime beef rib
dripping or lard
seasoning, salt, ground pepper

Preheat the oven at 240°C (475°F, Gas Mark 9) for 15 minutes. Preheat a shallow roasting tin with dripping or lard.

In turn, place the rib on both ends in the hot fat to seal the meat, then place it fat side up. Cook for 25–30 minutes at that temperature, then lower the oven to 180°C (350°F, Gas Mark 4).

Continue to roast for 1 hour without basting, then baste at regular intervals until it is cooked to your liking — estimate total time 20 minutes to each 500 g (1 lb). Transfer the beef to a warm tray, ready for carving.

Serves 6

Serve with
Roast potatoes
Puree of carrot or swede
Cauliflower cheese

Roast Gravy

beef stock
red wine

Prepare a little beef stock beforehand with a few beef bones and diced carrots, celery, onion and leeks and a few white peppercorns. Remove scum and reduce by half.

If you follow the Chef's tip and make the Yorkshire Pudding in the roasting pan, you should make the gravy first so it can have some of the pan juices. Place the pan on the heat and deglaze with a glass of red wine. Reduce, add beef stock and simmer slowly, reducing by half. Season to taste.

When serving the Yorkshire Pudding, dip slices into the beef gravy for a few seconds before serving.

Yorkshire Pudding

1 cup (4 oz) plain flour
pinch salt
1 egg
300 ml (½ pint) milk, warm
30 g (1 oz) dripping or lard, melted

Sift flour and salt together in a bowl. Add the egg and a little milk, work into a smooth paste. Then add rest of the milk a little at a time. The batter should be smooth and free of lumps. Leave to stand for 20 minutes.

Heat the pans in the top of the oven at 220°C (425°F, Gas Mark 7). Put a little fat from the roast beef into each pan. Heat until smoking hot and pour in the Yorkshire Pudding batter. Bake for 25–30 minutes.

Chef's Tip: Remove the beef from the roasting pan and place it back in the oven at the top, on a rack. Throw off a little of the roasting fat, pour the batter into the tray, and cook it under the beef. All the juices from the meat will give the pudding a delicious flavour.

BARBARA RONAY (Britain)
Wife of Egon Ronay, restaurant critic

Vegetable Game Soup

1 large carrot
1 large leek
½ turnip
1 small onion
left-over pheasant, duck or chicken carcass
2 chicken stock cubes
2 cloves garlic, finely chopped
1 tablespoon finely chopped parsley
6 juniper berries, crushed
2 bay-leaves
¼ teaspoon thyme
¼ teaspoon sage
pinch of mace
salt and pepper to taste

    Finely slice the carrot, leek, turnip and onion. Bring a saucepan of water, large enough to hold the carcass, to the boil. Stir in the crumbled stock cubes and add all the ingredients. Cover and simmer gently for 1½ hours. Remove the carcass and bay-leaves before serving.

Caramel Mousse

8 egg whites
1 sachet plus ¾ teaspoon powdered gelatine
6 egg yolks
600 ml (1 pint) thickened (double) cream
1¼ cups (8 oz) castor sugar

    Beat the egg whites until stiff. Dissolve the gelatine in a little hot water. Carefully mix the egg yolks, cream and gelatine together.
    Place the sugar in a small saucepan and heat over a flame until caramelised. Plunge the saucepan immediately into cold water.
    Slowly beat the caramel into the cream mixture. Lightly fold in the egg whites and pour the mixture into a bowl for serving.
    Leave to stand in the refrigerator for a few hours before serving.

ROSALIND RUNCIE (Britain)
Wife of the Archbishop of Canterbury

Bacon Slipper Braise

4–5 kg (2–2½ lb) piece bacon slipper
1 medium onion, chopped
2 sticks celery, chopped
30 g (1 oz) lard
625 g (20 oz) tin baked beans
150 ml (¼ pint) water
pepper
¼ teaspoon mustard
tomato paste

Soak bacon well overnight. Drain and put into a 2.5 litre (4½ pint) casserole.
Fry onion and celery in lard, without browning, till tender (about 5 minutes). Stir in baked beans, water, pepper, mustard and some tomato paste. Bring to boil. Pour over bacon.
Cook in oven at 200°C (400°F, Gas Mark 6) for 1¼ hours.

Lou's Chocolate Munchies

250 g (8 oz) butter
1 cup (8 oz) sugar
2¾ cups (11 oz) flour
1 egg
15 g (½ oz) cocoa
1 teaspoon vanilla
1 egg yolk
30 g (1 oz) almonds, chopped
1 tablespoon sugar

Cream butter and sugar. Stir in flour, whole egg, cocoa and vanilla. Put in Swiss roll tin. Brush with beaten egg yolk. Sprinkle almonds mixed with sugar on top. Bake for 25 minutes in moderate oven.

SHREWSBURY SCHOOL (Britain)
From the Headmaster

Apple Vichyssoise

2 large potatoes
3–4 stalks celery
1–2 onions
2 dessert apples, peeled
600 ml (1 pint) chicken stock
1 tablespoon butter
salt and freshly ground pepper
1 teaspoon curry powder
300 ml (½ pint) thickened (double) cream
chives to garnish

Dice vegetables and apples and combine with stock in a large pan. Bring to boil and simmer for 15–20 minutes until tender. Liquidise. Return to pan adding seasoning, butter and curry powder and simmer for 5 minutes. Remove from heat and add cream.

Serve hot or cold, topped with chives.

MAUREEN SIMPSON (Australia)
Cookery writer

Australian Meat Pie

A family-style home-made meat pie.

Shortcrust Pastry
1 cup (4 oz) plain flour
½ cup (2 oz) self-raising flour
good pinch salt
100 g (3½ oz) cooking margarine or butter
¼ cup cold water
squeeze lemon juice (optional)

Place flours and salt in a mixing bowl, rub in margarine or butter with fingertips, and mix into a dough with water and lemon juice. Turn out on to a lightly floured surface and knead lightly with a little flour. Rest for 20 minutes before rolling.

Filling
3 rashers bacon, chopped
1 large onion, peeled and sliced
1.5 kg (3 lb) chuck steak
2 cups water
½ teaspoon ground black pepper
½–1 teaspoon salt
½ teaspoon dried thyme
1 stick celery, very finely diced
¼ cup (1 oz) plain flour

Fry the chopped bacon in a large heavy-based saucepan, and when the fat starts to melt add the onion. Lower heat and fry very gently for about 10 minutes (this develops the flavour of the onion).

Meanwhile, trim away all fat from the meat. Chop meat into tiny cubes and add to the pot with the water, pepper, salt, thyme and celery. Cover the pot and simmer gently for about 1½ hours or until meat is tender.

Mix flour with a little cold water, smoothing out any lumps. Add this to the meat mixture and stir until the mixture boils and thickens. Pour into a deep pie plate (2 litre (3½ pint) capacity). Place a pie funnel in the centre of the meat.

Roll out the pastry, cut a few strips for a collar and place these on the wet rim of the pie dish. Brush with milk or beaten egg. Lift remaining pastry on to a rolling-pin and place on top of the pie. Trim edges with a knife. Press edges together with a fork to seal. Make a few steam holes. Glaze with beaten egg or milk and bake in a hot oven for 30–40 minutes.

Serves 6–8

Australian Damper

Traditionally the Australian Damper is cooked in a camp oven buried in the ashes of the fire. This recipe is for making an Aussie Damper at home.

500 g (1 lb) self-raising flour
2 teaspoons salt
1 tablespoon sugar
1½ cups water or milk (or a mixture of both)
1 egg yolk mixed with 1 tablespoon milk

Sift flour and salt into a basin. Mix in the sugar then make a well in the centre of the mixture. Pour in water or milk and mix quickly into a soft dough. Empty out on to a lightly floured surface and knead lightly.

Place dough rounded side up into a well-greased 2 litre (3½ pint) casserole dish. Cut a deep cross in the top of the dough, then brush dough with beaten yolk and milk. Grease inside lid of casserole and cover the dish (or use greased foil).

Bake in a moderately hot oven for ½ hour then uncover and bake for a further 20–30 minutes. Stand for a few minutes then turn out of dish. Cut into thick slices and serve warm or cold with butter and golden syrup.

Crispy Chicken in Mango Sauce

4 chicken fillets
1 tablespoon plain flour
1 egg, beaten
dry breadcrumbs (or mixture dry breadcrumbs and finely chopped blanched almonds)
60 g (2 oz) butter for frying
1 mango
juice of 1 orange
pinch chilli powder or dash sweet chilli sauce

Dust chicken fillets lightly with flour, then dip into beaten egg and straight into crumbs (or mixture of crumbs and almonds). Press on firmly. Put butter into a frying-pan and melt gently, then add chicken fillets. Continue to cook over a fairly low heat (crumbs tend to burn easily, especially with almonds) until the chicken is cooked and coating is golden both sides, about 10 minutes (try not to overcook, chicken should be still juicy). Alternatively, if entertaining and don't wish to watch carefully, simply brown lightly in butter then transfer to a baking dish and cook in a moderate oven for about 20 minutes.

Puree flesh of mango in a food processor or blender, adding orange juice to thin to desired consistency. Spike with little chilli. Heat gently in a separate pan and serve as a sauce *under* the chicken on the plate.
Serves 4

Billy Tea

From *Australian Cuisine*

Hints for making a good brew
- The first and most important thing is to have a black billy. This is simply an aluminium or tin billy, blackened by the fire. Why black? It heats faster, a shiny surface would reflect the heat.
- Place a green gum stick across the open-topped billy to stop too much smoke getting into the water. A lid of course would do the same thing (as well as making billy boil faster), but traditionally the billy was an old jam tin or 'boulli beef can', hence the name.

- To stop the handle becoming too hot, always keep upright above the billy.
- When the water is boiling rapidly, throw in a handful of tea and remove from fire immediately.
- Now, this is the tricky bit. Hold the billy at arm's length and swing around in a complete circle. The purpose of this (apart from the theatrics) is to force the leaves to the bottom of the billy, leaving beautifully clear tea on top. For the faint-hearted, a few sharp taps on the side of the billy will do the same thing.

JAMES SMILLIE (Australia)
Actor

Curried Chicken

This is both very filling and very fulfilling — a cracker round the pool on hot days.

1 brown onion
2 tablespoons oil
1 tablespoon hot curry powder
1 teaspoon tomato puree
juice of 1 lemon
150 ml (¼ pint) chicken stock
2 tablespoons mango chutney
300 ml (½ pint) Hellmanns mayonnaise
1 chicken, roasted
boiled white long-grain rice
green pepper
spring onions
celery
hazelnuts
sultanas

Soften the onion in the oil. Add curry powder and cook for 2 minutes. Add tomato puree, lemon juice, chicken stock and mango chutney. Stir and simmer for 5 minutes. Let it cook and then put the mixture through a sieve. Fold in mayonnaise.

Break chicken into pieces and place in creamy mixture. Place the chicken in the centre of a large serving dish.

Finely dice peppers, spring onions and celery; mix with rice, hazelnuts and sultanas. Arrange in a border around the chicken.

Serve with avocado and green salad.

Note: This can be prepared the day before and kept in the refrigerator overnight.

DELIA SMITH (Britain)
Cookery writer

Cardinal Peaches

These look and taste stunning served in stemmed glass dishes — a really fresh and fragrant way to end a meal.

6 large ripe peaches
4½ teaspoons castor sugar
60–90 g (2–3 oz) icing sugar
1 vanilla pod

375 g (¾ lb) fresh raspberries
icing sugar
1 tablespoon flaked almonds

First wash the peaches and place them, whole and unpeeled, in a large saucepan. Pour in just enough water to cover them, add castor sugar and vanilla pod, bring to simmering point, then put a lid on and simmer gently for about 10 minutes. Drain the peaches, and when they're cold slip the skins off.

Meanwhile, sprinkle the raspberries with icing sugar and leave them for 20 minutes. Then press them through a nylon sieve to make a puree.

Place the peaches in a bowl, pour the raspberry puree over, cover with cling film and chill very thoroughly for several hours.

To serve, place in one large serving dish or in six individual dishes and sprinkle with flaked almonds.

MICHAEL SMITH (Britain)
Cookery writer

Chilled Redcurrant Souffle

It is quite in order to add gelatine to a mixture whisked over hot water — it won't boil and toughen. This dessert does not freeze.

250 g (½ lb) redcurrants
¼ cup (2 oz) sugar
¼ cup water
10 eggs, separated
¼ cup (2 oz) castor sugar
juice of 3 lemons
1 sachet gelatine crystals
300 ml (½ pint) thickened (double) cream, half-whipped
1 teaspoon carmine or cochineal

First make strong, thick redcurrant juice — simmer the redcurrants and sugar with the water until the mixture is reduced to a pulp. Strain and press through a fine sieve.

Place a large glass ceramic basin over a pan of boiling water and whisk the redcurrant juice, egg yolks, castor sugar, lemon juice and gelatine crystals together until the whisk leaves a distinct trail (use a balloon whisk).

Stand the basin in a sink of cold water and leave the mixture to cool but not set, stirring from time to time.

Mix the half-whipped cream well in. Mix in the colouring. Beat the egg whites until stiff. Whisk a third of the beaten whites well into the redcurrant mixture, then cut and fold in the rest.

Pour into a glass dish and cover with plastic film. Chill before serving.

Serves 10-12

DARYL SOMERS (Australia)
TV personality

Fresh Pasta with Smoked Trout and Red and Black Caviare
(Entree)

fresh home-made pasta, finely cut
1 smoked trout, cleaned well of skin and bones and chopped finely
2 tablespoons cream
salt and pepper
1 small jar each red and black lumpfish caviare

Cook pasta and drain. Place smoked trout into a saucepan with the cream and a little salt and pepper, and cook over moderate heat for 1 minute. Add pasta to saucepan and toss well to blend flavours.

Place a small pile of pasta on each plate. Decorate with a spoonful of red then black caviare. Serve immediately while hot with, perhaps, a magnum of champagne!

MARY STEELE (Australia)
Children's author

> The Australian diet isn't solely made up of meat pies, rump steak, barbecues and pavlovas! Because of our wide range of climatic regions and (since the 1950s) our rich multicultural society, we are fortunate in the huge variety of fresh fruits and vegetables available to us all the year round. What isn't grown locally is flown in fresh from the other States and regions.

Pumpkin Soup

Pumpkin is a popular and versatile vegetable in Australia, where several varieties are grown. The following recipe makes a satisfying and colourful winter soup.

60 g (2 oz) butter
1 large onion, chopped
1 kg (2 lb) pumpkin,
    cut into 5 cm (2 inch) chunks
600 ml (1 pint) milk
1½ cups water

2 chicken stock cubes
salt and pepper to taste
½ teaspoon allspice
½ cup dry sherry
chopped chives and cream

Melt butter in a large pan and fry onion gently for 10 minutes. Add pumpkin and continue frying for another 10 minutes, stirring frequently.
Add milk and simmer until pumpkin is soft. Blend or put through a sieve. Add water, stock cubes and seasoning.
Just before serving add the sherry. Serve with a swirl of cream and some chopped chives.
Serves 8

Note: Other vegetables can be added with the pumpkin — e.g. a potato, 2 stalks celery, a carrot, etc.

Red Fruit Salad

As Christmas in Australia coincides with summer, festive alternatives to hot plum puddings are often welcome. This recipe is ideal for a festive summer occasion.

Make a base of stewed red plums, using the minimum of water so as to produce a thick, fruity syrup. Allow to cool.

Shortly before the meal add to the plums a variety of other red fruits — e.g. strawberries, loganberries, raspberries, pitted cherries, balls of watermelon. Mix gently.

Quantities can be varied to suit the number of serves required and the fruits available. The watermelon is recommended for its attractive colour and its crunchy texture.

Serve alone or with cream or ice-cream.

Frozen Grapes

During the grape season select some bunches of firm, sweet, *seedless* grapes (sultanas). Wash and dry and cut into small branchlets. Place in a container in the deep freeze.

During the non-grape season these can be produced at dinner parties and served (still frozen) with cheese or dessert.

SIR NINIAN STEPHEN (Australia)
Governor-General of Australia

Yabby Mousse

150–300 g (5–10 oz) yabby (freshwater crayfish) meat (15–20 yabbies)
2 cups milk
little salt
3 teaspoons gelatine softened in ¼ cup cold water
300 ml (½ pint) (single) cream, whipped
2 egg whites, whipped
salt
sugar
lemon juice

Shell cooked yabbies and set the meat aside. Add shells to the milk and let simmer with a little salt for 15–30 minutes. Then add the softened gelatine to the milk and let it dissolve. Strain the milk through a fine sieve or cloth and let it cool to room temperature.

Pour milk into a blender, add the yabby meat, and puree until very fine. Pour the mixture into a large bowl and fold in the whipped cream and egg whites. Season to taste with salt, sugar and a little lemon juice. Pour mousse into moulds and let it set.

Serve with sorrel mayonnaise.

Sorrel Mayonnaise

1 cup mayonnaise
6–10 fresh sorrel leaves, chopped
salt
ground white pepper
sugar

Put mayonnaise into the blender, add sorrel leaves and blend until mayonnaise turns a nice green colour. Season to taste with salt, pepper and sugar.

JAN STEPHENSON (Australia)
Golf professional

Boiled Fruitcake

My favourite fruitcake, as it is always moist.

185 g (6 oz) margarine
1 cup (5 oz) brown sugar
1 kg (2 lb) mixed dried fruit
1 teaspoon nutmeg
1 teaspoon mixed spice
1 cup canned crushed pineapple, drained
1 cup pineapple juice
½ teaspoon bicarbonate of soda
2 eggs
1 cup (4 oz) plain flour
1 cup (4 oz) self-raising flour

Place margarine, sugar, mixed fruit, nutmeg, spice, pineapple and juice in saucepan and bring to boil. When boiling remove from stove, add bicarbonate of soda. Allow to cool slightly. When just warm add beaten eggs and flours.
Bake in moderately hot oven for 1½ hours.

Tuna Pie
(Luncheon Dish)

440 g (14 oz) can tuna
440 g (14 oz) can mushroom soup
½ green pepper
½ cup sour cream
mashed potato
salt and pepper

Combine drained tuna, mushroom soup and chopped pepper. Pour into lightly greased pie dish.
Mix sour cream with mashed potato and salt and pepper. Spoon potato mixture over tuna. Bake in moderately hot oven 30 minutes.

DAME JOAN SUTHERLAND (Australia)
Opera singer

Leg of Lamb with Apricot and Rice Stuffing

2–2.5 kg (4–5 lb) leg of lamb
salt and pepper
250 g (8 oz) long-grain rice
125 g (4 oz) dried apricots, soaked and chopped
30 g (1 oz) seeded raisins
30 g (1 oz) slivered almonds
1 teaspoon powdered cinnamon
1 teaspoon powdered coriander
1½ teaspoons powdered ginger
90 g (3 oz) melted butter

Bone, or ask butcher to bone, leg of lamb, leaving the shank intact.

Spread meat on board, making incisions in thickest parts. Season well with salt and pepper.

Boil the rice in a large pan with 1.8 litres (3 pints) water and 2 tablespoons salt until tender but still slightly firm. Drain well. Add apricots, raisins, almonds, cinnamon, coriander and ginger. Season, if needed, with more salt and pepper. Lay about half this mixture on to the lamb, roll meat and tie securely with string.

Lay the lamb on a rack in a roasting pan. Brush generously with melted butter, season with salt and pepper. Roast for 20 minutes per 500 g (1 lb), in an oven pre-heated to 190°C (375°F, Gas Mark 5). When cooked, remove to a warm plate and keep warm in a low oven.

Remove the fat from the pan juices, and stir the juices into the remaining rice and fruit mixture. Arrange the rice around the lamb before serving.

Serves 8–10

Papaw or Mango Water Ice or Sorbet

⅔ cup (5 oz) sugar (less may be preferred)
½ cup water
2 cups pureed papaw or mango
1½ tablespoons lemon or lime juice

Put sugar and water into a small saucepan and bring slowly to the boil until the sugar has dissolved. Boil for 5 minutes. Cool.

Add lemon or lime juice to the papaw/mango. Mix well with the cooled syrup. Pour into an ice tray and cover. Freeze until solid around the edges and mushy in the centre.

Remove to a cold bowl and beat until smooth. Return to tray, cover, and freeze again until solid, which usually takes about 3–4 hours. For a sorbet, add stiffly beaten white of egg before mixture has completely frozen. Remove the ice about 30 minutes before serving, to soften.
Serves 4

BEVERLEY SUTHERLAND SMITH (Australia)
Cookery writer

> Although these recipes are not Australian in the context of being pavlova or crayfish, which seem to be the two main things which distinguish our cuisine, they represent what I believe to be typical of this country — fresh food prepared in ways that leave in true flavours and are not too difficult.

Delight of the Gourmet

> This recipe was inspired by the way a Chicken Kiev is prepared. A section of flavoured butter, placed in the centre of a fillet steak, gradually melts as the meat is cooked and soaks into the beef, making it one of the juiciest and most flavoursome fillets imaginable. You can completely prepare it 12 hours beforehand, but it must be cooked at the last moment.

6 thick pieces of fillet steak, trimmed of all fat and sinew
60 g (2 oz) butter
2 tablespoons finely chopped parsley
1 clove garlic, crushed
pinch salt and a generous sprinkle of black pepper
French or Dijon mustard
plain flour
1 large egg beaten with 1 tablespoon oil
breadcrumbs made from stale white or brown bread
2 tablespoons vegetable or peanut oil
30 g (1 oz) butter

Using a sharp knife cut into the centre of the meat, turning it around to remove a small cylinder so it is like a case, but be careful not to pierce the base. Keep aside until you have done this to all the meat.

Mash the butter, parsley, garlic, salt and pepper until well blended. Push a portion of this butter into the centre hole of each steak and then replace the piece of meat you removed. Press down firmly. If it looks uneven form gently into a circle again; this is easy as fillet steak is quite pliable.

Spread a little mustard on top of each steak and dip each one into first the flour, then the beaten egg, and lastly coat with crumbs, pressing them on all sides. The amount you need will depend on the size of the steaks, and you may find you need some extra egg if they are large. Leave refrigerated for at least 1 hour for the butter and coating to firm.

Heat the oil and butter and when very hot cook on both sides, browning lightly. Don't have the heat too high or the crumbs will go brown before the meat is cooked. Usually they take about 4–5 minutes on each side, but timing will be a matter of personal taste.

Drain on some kitchen paper and serve immediately. It is lovely with a potato gratin baked with some cream and either a tossed green salad or baby green beans cooked in a simple manner.

Serves 6

Pears Alicia

A wonderful dish because, not only does it go well with almost any dinner, except of course one which has included some fruit with the meat, but it keeps beautifully and in fact improves by leaving to stand and mature for several days. Golden and translucent in colour, perfumed with orange, it can be served plain or accompanied by a little running cream.

6 slightly underripe eating pears of any variety
1 cup water
1 cup (7 oz) sugar
1 cup sweet sherry
peel of 1 orange, cut into strips and without any white pith
¼ cup brandy
¼ cup orange-flavoured liqueur

Peel the pears but leave on the stalks. Place the water, sugar, sherry and orange peel in a large pot. When the sugar has dissolved, add the pears and turn them over so they have liquid on the exposed sides or they will discolour. Cook over a very gentle heat until tender, turning them every so often. The slower they cook the better the flavour. They should become golden and glazed. When tender, remove and cool.

Chill, if keeping for days, turning them each day so the pears on top are underneath, completely covered with juice.

The day you are serving them add the brandy and liqueur. If added when they are first cooked it tends to evaporate away. If this amount of alcohol sounds too much you can reduce it to suit your own taste.

Serves 6

MAGGIE TABBERER (Australia)
Fashion Editor, *The Australian Women's Weekly*

Stuffed Chicken Breasts

This is a terrific summer dish I found in one of my cookbooks. The quantities shown will serve 24 as part of a buffet. Just divide according to the numbers you wish to feed, but it's yummy and I never seem to have any left over.

Chicken breasts are boned and split and the skin left on. A rich savoury filling is stuffed under the skin, the edges are tucked under, and the whole is baked for 30 minutes. These are delicious hot, warm or cold, whole or sliced. They are relatively inexpensive, large quantities can be made easily, and they can be stuffed and baked the day ahead of an event.

2 medium onions, finely chopped
2 tablespoons butter
2 x 315 g (10 oz) packages frozen chopped spinach, thawed and drained
1 kg (2 lb) whole milk ricotta cheese
2 eggs, slightly beaten
½ cup coarsely chopped parsley
2 tablespoons fresh oregano, summer savoury, chervil, etc.
salt and freshly ground pepper
nutmeg to taste
16 half chicken breasts (order the chicken boned, split, with the skin on)

Saute the onions in butter until soft. Combine with the other ingredients (except chicken) and mix well. Season highly.

Place each half breast skin side up on a board. Trim away excess fat. Loosen skin from one side and stuff approximately ⅓ cup of the filling under the skin. Tuck the skin and meat under the breast, forming an even, round, dome shape. Put the stuffed breasts in a buttered baking dish.

Fifteen minutes before baking pre-heat oven to 180°C (350°F, Gas Mark 4). Bake breasts until golden brown, about 30–35 minutes. Don't overcook or chicken will be dry. Cool slightly before serving, and cool to room temperature if you are going to slice into smaller serving pieces. Arrange on platters and decorate with fresh herbs.

NICK TATE (Australia)
Actor

Ho Yau Mun Gai
(Cold Chicken in Oyster Sauce)

1 chicken
celery leaves
1 onion
2 tablespoons honey
1 tablespoon oyster sauce
1 tablespoon soy sauce
½ teaspoon salt
¼ teaspoon five spice powder
3 tablespoons finely chopped spring onion
3 teaspoons finely grated fresh ginger
2 tablespoons sesame seeds

Put chopped onion and celery leaves in cold water with chicken. Bring slowly to boil, cover and simmer for 15–20 minutes. Turn off heat, let it cool in its own liquid (very important). When cold remove chicken and remove meat from bones.

Mix the honey, oyster sauce, soy sauce, salt and five spice powder in a bowl. Combine it with the meat from the chicken and leave at least 30 minutes (up to 2 hours is safe — too long and the meat goes a bit soggy).

Before serving sprinkle the spring onions and ginger over it. Finally, just before serving, roast the sesame seeds in a saucepan over heat until they start to turn brown (watch them closely, a fraction too long and they will burn). Sprinkle the hot sesame seeds over the dish and mix up.

Serve this with dry fried rice, lightly sprinkled with nuts (e.g. cashews and pecans), together with fresh salad of predominantly chopped celery, carrots, cucumber, alfalfa and sultanas. Sliced fruit on the side — papaw, mango, banana and apple.

God my mouth's watering!

MARGARET THATCHER (Britain)
Prime Minister of Great Britain

Orange and Walnut Cake

250 g (8 oz) self-raising flour
½ teaspoon salt
185 g (6 oz) butter
¾ cup (6 oz) castor sugar
3 large eggs
rind of 1 orange
30 g (1 oz) mixed peel, chopped
60 g (2 oz) walnuts
1 tablespoon concentrated orange juice

Sift flour and salt together. Cream the butter and sugar and add beaten eggs. Add half the flour and the other ingredients and blend. Add the rest of the flour.

Spoon the mixture into an 18 cm (7 inch) greased cake tin and cook in a pre-heated moderate oven for 1¼ hours.

Icing
250 g (8 oz) icing sugar
2–3 tablespoons concentrated orange juice

Warm icing sugar and concentrated orange juice together in a pan until smooth. Ice the cake with this mixture while icing is still warm. Be careful not to over-heat the icing when blending.

BRIGITTE TILLERAY (Britain)
Cookery writer

My first taste of England and English food goes back to my childhood when we used to visit Tante Jacqueline, the English bride my French uncle had married during the war.

There was something magical about the chintzy atmosphere of their house, the copper kettle by the fireplace, the Christmas crackers and their bright trinkets, the mid-afternoon tea — all small details which seemed so foreign at the time. Little was I to know then that a few years later I would make my home in England and it would all become so familiar.

Jacqueline was a fabulous cook and introduced us to many delectable English dishes. I have fond memories of her Stilton Souffle and of her Charlotte au Whisky, a dessert she created as a culinary compromise: a traditional French chocolate delight laced with her favourite drink.

Stilton Souffle

60 g (2 oz) butter
75 g (2½ oz) flour
450 ml (¾ pint) milk
110 g (3½ oz) stilton

¼ cup (2 oz) chopped walnuts
¼ cup (2 oz) chopped celery
5 eggs, separated
salt and pepper to taste

Preheat the oven at 220°C (425°F, Gas Mark 7). In a large pan over low heat melt the butter, then add the flour. Mix constantly with a wooden spoon until the mixture is frothy. Pour the milk at once and stir until the mixture thickens. As soon as the mixture starts bubbling take away from the heat.

Add the crumbled cheese, walnuts and celery, then the egg yolks one by one, mixing well. Beat the egg whites until very firm, fold them softly into the mixture. Pour into a buttered souffle dish and cook in the oven for 40–45 minutes, making sure you don't open the oven in between. Serve at once.

Serves 4

Charlotte au Whisky

220 g (7 oz) plain chocolate
220 g (7 oz) unsalted butter
2 teaspoons castor sugar

2 eggs
24 sponge fingers (or equivalent)
2 large measures whisky

Melt the chocolate over low heat, adding a little water if necessary. Add the butter bit by bit, stirring all the time, then the castor sugar. Leave to cool.

Separate the egg yolks from the whites. Add the yolks to the chocolate mixture. Whisk the whites until firm and fold them into the mixture.

Line a charlotte dish or souffle dish with the biscuits soaked in whisky and water (the strength of the liquid is entirely your choice). Fill with the chocolate mousse. Refrigerate overnight.

The following day turn on to a serving dish, serve with cream or *sauce anglaise*.

ADELE WEISS (Australia)
Fashion designer

Pumpkin Soup

Just everyone loves my pumpkin soup! I love a touch of garlic — only a very small amount should be added to vegetables when boiling.

1 kg (2 lb) pumpkin	salt and pepper
185 g (6 oz) potatoes	¼ cup (2 oz) rice (optional)
125 g (4 oz) onions	600 ml (1 pint) salted water
250 g (8 oz) tomatoes	1 teaspoon butter
2.4 litres (4 pints) water	2 large tablespoons cream

Peel and cut up pumpkin, potatoes, onions and tomatoes. Put in saucepan with the water, salt and pepper. Bring to boil and cook until soft — roughly 25–30 minutes.

While vegetables are cooking boil rice in salted water. This may be deleted and croutons used instead. When rice is cooked, strain and rinse with cold water.

Allow vegetable mixture to cool down completely, then put in liquidiser till all creamy. Return to saucepan, heat gently. Add the rice, butter and cream.

Soup should be a rich, creamy consistency.

Colonial Curd Cake

I first made this cheesecake in 1963 and it's still my favourite.

Pastry

60 g (2 oz) soft butter	1 egg yolk
2 tablespoons sugar	1¼ cups (5 oz) plain flour

Cream the butter with the sugar, mix in the egg yolk then the flour. Butter a 20 cm (8 inch) springform tin and line the base and sides with the pastry (I usually just press it in).

Filling

500 g (1 lb) cottage cheese	2 tablespoons milk
45 g (1½ oz) soft butter	4 eggs, separated
⅔ cup (5 oz) sugar	6 teaspoons cornflour
½ teaspoon vanilla	½ cup cream
grated rind of 1 lemon	whipped cream and nutmeg

Force the cheese through a sieve and set aside.

In another bowl cream the butter with half the sugar, mix in the vanilla and lemon rind. Add the remaining sugar and the milk. Mix well and beat in the egg yolks with the cornflour, then the sieved cheese in alternate lots with the cream. Fold in the stiffly beaten egg whites and turn into the pastry-lined tin.

Bake the cake in a hot oven — 220°C (425°F, Gas Mark 7) — until the top edge of the pastry begins to brown (about 10 minutes). Then reduce the heat to 180°C (350°F, Gas Mark 4) or very moderate. Cook 50 minutes more, or until nearly set in the centre. Turn off the heat and leave in the oven another 15 minutes. Cool before removing the sides of the tin.

Cover with whipped cream and sprinkle with nutmeg (although it's still delicious without these). It's best if chilled until next day.

Walnut Cream Cake

5 eggs
½ cup (4 oz) castor sugar
90 g (3 oz) ground walnuts
½ cup (2 oz) plain flour

Separate 3 eggs. Beat yolks with 2 whole eggs until light and creamy. Slowly add sugar and beat until dissolved. Lightly fold in ground walnuts and sifted flour.

Beat remaining 3 egg whites until peaks are firm. Lightly fold into walnut mixture. Pour into 2 greased and lined 20 cm (8 inch) sandwich tins. Bake in moderate oven 25–30 minutes or until cake comes away slightly from the sides of tins.

When cake is cold join with Coffee Rum Cream. Spread cream over top and sides and decorate with walnut halves. A little melted chocolate may also be spread on the top.

Coffee Rum Cream

450 ml (¾ pint) cream
⅓ cup (3 oz) sugar
2 teaspoons instant coffee
2 teaspoons rum

Combine and beat until light, soft peaks form.

WESTERN AUSTRALIA HOUSE, London

A Selection of Australian Recipes

Australian food has a character of its own. Recipes have developed from European and Asian tastes adapted to a climate that varies from a tropical north to a temperate south. Advantage has also been taken of the island continent's wide varieties of high-quality food, including meat, fruits, vegetables and shellfish, to improve on the tastes introduced by migrants, visitors and students from other nations.

Australia is fortunate in having a wide selection of tropical fruits such as mangoes, passionfruit, pineapples, papaw, custard apples and bananas. Canned and dried fruits are also plentiful and of high quality. Australian wines are among the finest in the world. We recommend that you serve them as an excellent complement to a well-cooked meal.

Grapefruit and Seafood Cocktail

4 medium-sized grapefruit
1 teaspoon dry sherry or lemon juice
½ teaspoon salad oil
1 cup mixed seafood (lobster, crab, prawns)
salt and cayenne pepper
mayonnaise

Cut tops off grapefruit about one-third down. With a curved fruit knife cut all round the grapefruit to remove the pulp, cutting out centre core and seeds. Dice fruit and put into bowl with sherry and oil.

Dice the lobster, shell and halve the prawns, flake the crab (if preferred use only lobster). Mix with grapefruit. Season to taste, mixing well, then fill grapefruit cases with this mixture. If coral from the lobster is available, chop it finely and sprinkle on each grapefruit as a garnish. Serve mayonnaise separately.

For a simpler cocktail, substitute flaked, canned salmon for the seafood above.
Serves 4

Lamb Crown Roast with Fruit Stuffing

2 kg (4–4½ lb) loin of lamb shaped into a crown
60 g (2 oz) dried apricots, soaked overnight
90 g (3 oz) prunes, soaked overnight
1 cooking apple
8–10 cherries
45 g (1½ oz) nuts
2 cups (4 oz) breadcrumbs

parsley
300 ml (½ pint) stock, or water with stock cubes
grated rind and juice of ½ lemon
1 tablespoon oil or melted butter
1 small can halved apricots for garnish

Protect the tip of each rib with foil and brush the whole loin with a little oil.

Mix all ingredients for the stuffing. Place in the centre of the loin and cook for 1½ hours in a moderately hot oven.

When cooked, remove foil. Place crown roast in a serving dish and keep warm while making gravy.

Passionfruit Pavlova

This could almost be considered Australia's national dish — it is certainly the best known all over Australia. The story is that it was evolved by a well-known hostess who was entertaining the famous ballerina, Pavlova, during her tour of Australia, and named it after her famous guest. Certainly other countries know the delicious meringue pie, but they cannot use our passionfruit as a filling; and it is the combination of light meringue crust, whipped cream and passionfruit which makes it so deservedly popular.

There are a few rules to observe when making a pavlova, but it is really quite simple once you remember these. Never use eggs straight from ice-box or refrigerator. Stand them in the kitchen for some time before whipping. They should be at room temperature for best results. Be sure both mixing bowl and beater are thoroughly dry and not too cold. You can use castor sugar, or a mixture of castor and granulated sugars, but be sure they are free of lumps. Castor sugar is best sifted before using.

Prepare a foundation for the meringue by brushing a sheet of thick white paper over with salad oil then placing it on a cold oven slide, or by lining a pie plate with oiled paper. It is a good idea to draw a circle on the paper before oiling to use as a guide when shaping the meringue. The paper should peel off quite easily after cooking.

The basic formula is to allow ¼ cup (2 oz) sugar to each egg white. Here is the recipe for a pavlova to serve 6 or 7.

4 egg whites
½ cup (4 oz) castor sugar
½ cup (4 oz) granulated sugar
½ teaspoon white vinegar
1 teaspoon cornflour
300 ml (½ pint) thickened (double) cream
passionfruit

Beat the egg whites until stiff but not dry — you should be able to turn the basin upside down without the egg whites moving. Now start adding the sugar 2 tablespoons at a time, beating well between each addition, until sugar is dissolved and the texture is thick and chalky white. Now add the vinegar gradually and sift the cornflour over the mixture, folding in gently but thoroughly.

Turn the mixture on to a paper-lined tray, forming into a round and slightly hollowing out the middle. Put into coolest part of oven which has been pre-heated to 140°C (275°F, Gas Mark 1) and bake for 1½–2 hours. Be careful the pavlova does not colour too much. When crisp remove from oven and carefully remove paper. Be very careful when handling, as it is brittle while hot. Place on serving plate and cool thoroughly.

When ready to serve whip cream until thick, then fold in passionfruit pulp and fill pavlova. Or, if preferred, fill meringue case with ice cream and pour passionfruit over the top. Serve at once.

Strawberries or other berries may also be used, or a good fruit salad mixture.

Anzac Biscuits

185 g (6 oz) rolled oats
185 g (6 oz) plain flour
185 g (6 oz) desiccated coconut
185 g (6 oz) brown or white sugar
1½ teaspoons baking powder
220 g (7 oz) butter
2 tablespoons golden syrup

Mix all dry ingredients together in a bowl. Melt the butter, pour over the flour mixture and add the syrup. Shape into small balls. Flatten them with a fork on to a buttered baking sheet and bake at 150°C (300°F, Gas Mark 2) until done — about 15 minutes.

Recipes from the Outback

Mostly for interest, here are a few suggestions from the Australian outback. While you may hesitate to serve blue-tongued lizard, you may care to taste kangaroo tail.

Damper

Take 1½ kg (3 lb) flour and throw it into a dish, put a bit of salt into it and some rising — 30 g (1 oz) cream of tartar and 15 g (½ oz) bicarbonate of soda. Pour some water into the dish and mix it well into a light dough. Now sprinkle a little flour over the bottom of the camp oven to prevent the damper sticking, put in the dough and put the lid on.

To cook, place into a shallow hole in the ground into which hot ashes have been placed with a shovel. Put the camp oven over the hot ashes, then cover it completely with more hot ashes. Cook for about 30 minutes. If the camp oven is tapped and gives off a hollow sound, the damper is done.

Sinkers

Using the same basic dough as for damper, make it into round balls the size of a tennis ball. Put them into boiling water with a bit of fat on top, which helps to seal the dough. Boil for 15 minutes. Good served hot with honey.

Witchetty Grubs

All you have to do is cut them out from the trees and cook them over the coals, or in a frying-pan with a dab of butter to give them an extra flavour.

Blue-Tongued Lizard

First catch your lizard. Before it is cooked it is placed on the fire and turned over until all the scales become crisp. The entrails are then carefully drawn out with an expert twist. When it is clean, make an incision under the forearm. The reptile is cooked lengthways in a ground oven. The best parts are the ribs and the arms.

Baked Kangaroo Tail

First remove the hair from the skin, which must be left on the tail. After cleaning, cut into pieces the width of the cooking pot. Lay the pieces in the pot with some water, to which a little fat and some salt have been added, and bake in a hot oven. Kangaroo tail is very good baked in the ashes; and some outback sheep- and cattlemen are most enthusiastic about kangaroo tail cooked in a ground oven with the hide still on it.

How to Bake a Snake

If a snake is killed and thrown straight on to the fire, it immediately twists and turns into a very disconcerting shape indeed. To cook it properly you need a fire and two people. They sit one each side of the fire and stretch the snake over the heat, passing it to and fro slowly.

TERRY WOGAN (Britain)
TV personality

Chicken and Asparagus Casserole

6 chicken breasts
chicken stock
1 large tin green asparagus spears
1 tin condensed mushroom soup
300 ml (½ pint) thickened (double) cream
2 tablespoons medium sherry
¼ cup (1 oz) cheddar cheese, grated
paprika

   Gently poach chicken breasts in a little chicken stock for approximately 15 minutes.
   Grease a shallow casserole dish that will take the chicken breasts in one layer. Place the drained asparagus on the bottom of the dish. Place the chicken breasts on top.
   Combine soup, cream and sherry in a saucepan and heat gently, stirring constantly. Pour over chicken and asparagus. Sprinkle the grated cheese and paprika over. Season to taste.
   Bake in a hot oven 200°C (400°F, Gas Mark 6) for 20 minutes.

CLIFF YOUNG (Australia)
Marathon runner and farmer

Mashed Potato

Cliff likes the simple, uncomplicated things in life, including food. He loves wholesome, natural food and dislikes too many 'mixtures' and food overdone. Cliff's mother used to make this recipe for him.   Mary Young

Simply add finely chopped onion, parsley, garlic, salt and pepper to potatoes mashed with butter and milk. Quantities according to taste.

Index

Ackee and Salt Fish 77
Anzac Biscuits 61, 124
  with Peanuts 30
Apple Vichyssoise 102
Apricot Mustard Glazed Corned
  Silverside 94
Armenian Soup 49
Aunty Glad's Cornish Pasty 90
Australian Damper 103
Australian Meat Pie 102
Australian Roast Lamb with Mint
  Glazed Pears 12
Avocado and Grapefruit Salad 14
Avocado Cocktail 26
Bachelor Scrambled Eggs and
  Tomatoes 69
Bacon and Tomato Topping 86
Bacon Slipper Braise 101
Baked Kangaroo Tail 125
Baked Snake 15
Baked Tasmanian Atlantic Salmon 12
Barbecue, State-of-the-Art 76
Basil Butter 54, 86
Basil Sauce 13
Beef
  and Mushroom Pie with
    Cheesy Suet Crust 53
  Australian Meat Pie 102
  Delight of the Gourmet 113
  Macho Olives 32
  Manor House 82
  Oriental 85
  Prime Roast Rib 98
  Spicy Curry 94
Beppi's Mozzarella Salad and Basil
  Sauce 13
Billy Tea 104
Biscuit Tortoni 39
Biscuits
  Anzac 61, 124
  Anzac with Peanuts 30
  Millet and Peanut Cookies 51
Blue-Tongued Lizard 125
Boiled Fruitcake 111
Bolognese Sauce a la Alan 74
Bran Muffins 40
Bread and Butter Pudding 23
Bygraves Special 37
Cakes
  Boiled Fruitcake 111
  Colonial Curd 120
  Great Carrot Wedding 24
  Jaffa Lamingtons 27
  Lamingtons 18
  Lamingtons 'Bessie's Beauties' 73
  Orange and Walnut 117
  Sponge 30
  Swiss Roll 88
  Walnut Cream 121

Caper Sauce 42
Caramel Mousse 100
Cardinal Peaches 106
Carpetbag Sausages 12
Carpetbag Steak 11
Caviare Profiteroles 34
Charlotte au Whisky 119
Cheesy Crusted Leg of Lamb 65
Chicken
  and Asparagus Casserole 126
  Cold, in Oyster Sauce 116
  Crispy, in Mango Sauce 104
  Curried 105
  Mustard Seed with
    Spring Vegetables 64
  Stuffed Breasts 115
  with Orange Sauce 58
Chilled Redcurrant Souffle 106
Chinese Pepper Steak with Rice 38
Chrysanthemum Duck 43
Cocktail Sauce 10
Coffee Rum Cream 121
Cold Chicken in Oyster Sauce 116
Colonial Curd Cake 120
Corned Silverside 75
  Apricot Mustard Glazed 94
Cornish Burnt Cream 92
Cornish Pasty 90
Coupe Juli 48
Crab, Dressed 95
Crayfish, Grilled Tails with Basil
  Butter 54
Creamy Leek Croustade 50
Crispy Chicken in Mango Sauce 104
Crispy Vegetarian Wuntuns 72
Crunchies 27
Crusty Cheese Damper 87
Cumquat Rice 68
Curried Chicken 105
Custard 29, 89
Damper 16, 124
  Australian 103
  Crusty Cheese 87
Delight of the Gourmet 113
Devilled Steak 34
Dressed Crab 95
Dried Fruit Salad 54
Duck, Chrysanthemum 43
Egg and Bacon Pie 11
Eggs
  Leo's Breakfast 80
  Scrambled, and Tomatoes 69
Fish in Lemon Butter 40
Flo's Pumpkin Scones 30
Florence's Anzac Biscuits with
  Peanuts 30
French Onion Soup 70
Fresh Fruit with Coconut Dipping
  Cream 66

Fresh Pasta with Smoked Trout and
  Red and Black Caviare 107
Frozen Grapes 109
Fruit Salad 18, 109
Fruity Shepherds Pie 93
Globe Artichokes with Mango Ginger
  Mayonnaise 66
Governor Phillip's Rum Pie 17
Grapefruit and Seafood Cocktail 1
Grapes, Frozen 109
Great Carrot Wedding Cake 24
Grilled Crayfish Tails with Basil
  Butter 54
Guinea Fowl Broth, Enhanced with
  Tarragon and Forest Mushrooms
Ham and Egg Pasta Savoury 77
Ho Yau Mun Gai 116
Hot Raspberry and Redcurrant
  Tarts 45
How to Bake a Snake 125
Ice-cream
  Biscuit Tortoni 39
  Strawberry 59
Iced Minted Green Pea Soup 10
Iced Prawn Cream Soup 51
Impossible Quiche 82
Jaffa Lamingtons 27
Kangaroo, Baked Tail 125
Khoshaf (Dried Fruit Salad) 54
Lamb
  Cheesy Crusted Leg 65
  Crown Roast with Fruit Stuffing
    en Croute with Fresh Figs
    and Ginger 22
  Leg with Apricot and
    Rice Stuffing 112
  Roast with Mint Glazed Pears 12
  Spit Roast Leg with Vegetables 60
  Wagga Wagga Beer Chops 52
Lamingtons 18
  'Bessie's Beauties' 73
  Jaffa 27
Leek and Noodle Casserole 41
Leg of Lamb with Apricot and Rice
  Stuffing 112
Lemon Delicious 43
Lemon Mayonnaise 96
Lemon Up and Down Pudding 59
Leo's Breakfast 80
Likky Soup 89
Lou's Chocolate Munchies 101
Macadamia Pumpkin 79
Macho Beef Olives 32
Mango Ginger Mayonnaise 66
Mango Water Ice or Sorbet 112
Manor House Beef 82
Marinated Scallops in Bacon 36
Mashed Potato 126

Mayonnaise
  Lemon 96
  Mango Ginger 66
  Sorrel 110
Meringues 63
Millet and Peanut Cookies 51
Minestrone 33
Mint Glazed Pears 12
Miracle Pie 83
Mother Bell's Custard 29
Muesli Fingers 31
Mum's Fruit Salad 18
Mustard Sauce 42
Mustard Seed Chicken with Spring Vegetables 64
Orange and Walnut Cake 117
Oriental Beef 85
Oysters 10
  with Three Toppings 86
Pancakes with Bechamel Vegetable Sauce 81
Papaw or Mango Water Ice or Sorbet 112
Passionfruit Pavlova 123
Pasta with Smoked Trout and Red and Black Caviare 107
Pavlova 25, 55, 61
  Passionfruit 123
Peaches, Cardinal 106
Pears
  Alicia 114
  Mint Glazed 12
  Stuffed 26
Pies (savoury)
  Australian Meat 102
  Beef and Mushroom with Cheesy Suet Crust 53
  Egg and Bacon 11
  Fruity Shepherds 93
  Steak and Kidney 28
  Tuna 111
Pies (sweet)
  Governor Phillip's Rum 17
  Miracle 83
  Pineapple and Mango 78
Pineapple and Mango Pie 78
Piquant Tomato Sauce 42
Pizza 74
Poisson Alfresco 57
Potato, Mashed 126
Prawn Kebabs 52
Prawns 10

Prime Roast Rib of Scottish Beef with Yorkshire Pudding 98
Puddings
  Bread and Butter 23
  Lemon Up and Down 59
  Sago Plum 29
  Seven-Cup 63
Pumpkin Scones 30
Pumpkin Soup 108, 120
Queensland Salad 14
Quiche, Impossible 82
Rabbit Venison 46
Rainbow Trout 62
Rainbow Vegetables in Lettuce Cups 71
Red Fruit Salad 109
Roast Gravy 99
Rustie's Aphrodisiac 79
Sago Plum Pudding 29
Salads
  Avocado and Grapefruit 14
  Beppi's Mozzarella 13
  Coupe Juli 48
  of Many Lettuces 15
  Queensland 14
  Scallop with Asparagus 21
  White Cabbage and Orange 49
Salmon
  Baked Tasmanian Atlantic 12
  in Vine Leaves 20
Sauces
  Basil 13
  Bolognese a la Alan 74
  Caper 42
  Cocktail 10
  Mustard 42
  Piquant Tomato 42
Sausages, Carpetbag 12
Savoury Steak and Noodles 83
Savoury Vegetable Casserole 58
Scallops
  Marinated, in Bacon 36
  Salad with Asparagus 21
Seafood and Grapefruit Cocktail 122
Seafood and Soft Cheese Lasagne 19
Seven-Cup Pudding 63
Shrimps in Avocado Nest with Cherry Tomato Eggs 64
Sinkers 125
Snake
  Baked 15
  How to Bake 125
Sorrel Mayonnaise 110

Souffles
  Chilled Redcurrant 106
  Stilton 118
Soupe de Poisson 47
Soups
  Apple Vichyssoise 102
  Armenian 49
  French Onion 70
  Guinea Fowl Broth 97
  Iced Minted Green Pea 10
  Iced Prawn Cream 51
  Likky 89
  Pumpkin 108, 120
  Soupe de Poisson 47
  Stilton 37
  Vegetable 62
  Vegetable Game 100
Sour Cream Topping 86
Spicy Beef Curry 94
Spit Roast Leg of Lamb with Vegetables 60
Sponge Cake 30
Squab Pie 91
State-of-the-Art Barbecue 76
Steak
  and Kidney Pie 28
  Carpetbag 11
  Chinese Pepper 38
  Devilled 34
  Savoury 83
Stilton Souffle 118
Stilton Soup 37
Strawberries in Melting Snow Kisses 67
Strawberry Ice-Cream 59
Stuffed Chicken Breasts 115
Stuffed Pears 26
Swiss Roll 88
Terrine of Oranges with Raspberry Sauce 56
Tongues a la Tony 42
Tony Barber's 'Porky Dogs' 28
Tropical Trifle 88
Trout, Rainbow 62
Tuna Casserole 84
Tuna Pie 111
Vegetable Game Soup 100
Vegetable Soup 62
Wagga Wagga Beer Chops 52
Walnut Cream Cake 121
White Cabbage and Orange Salad 49
Witchetty Grubs 125
Yabby Mousse 110
Yorkshire Pudding 98